T0334266

"In a casual, conversational style, Dr. Michael Reiter tells the story of family therapy. For the newly interested and beginning therapist, Reiter introduces the history, ethics, theorists, and the models that evolved since family therapy began in the 1950's. For the experienced family therapist, this book will be a reminder of the people and situations that built our profession. This title might say basic, but the content is anything but."

Wade Luquet, Ph.D., LCSW, *Gwynedd Mercy University.*
Author of Short-Term Couples Therapy: The Imago
Model in Action.

"By sticking to the nuts and bolts while providing important contextual knowledge, Dr. Michael Reiter has simplified marriage and family therapy and brought fresh insight to a new generation of readers who can transform the field of study going forward."

Dr. Kelsey Railsback, **LMFT,** *Touro University Worldwide,*
USA; Associate Professor, MFT Program.

FAMILY THERAPY

Family Therapy: The Basics provides a clear and concise overview of the field of family therapy and its foundational models. This text explores the history, skills, and theories upon which family therapy rests, highlighting the main figures, concepts, ethical principles, and methods. Focusing on the breadth of the field, readers are provided answers to some of the most important questions for potential therapists:

*   What are the primary skills family therapists use to help families change?
*   How do family therapists incorporate aspects of diversity into their practice?
*   What are the major models of family therapy practice?
*   Where is the field of family therapy headed in the future?

Family Therapy: The Basics is an ideal introduction for students exploring the field of psychotherapy and how a focus on the family and the use of various family therapy theories can help shift family organizations and relationships.

Michael D. Reiter, Ph.D., is a licensed marriage and family therapist in the state of Florida and an AAMFT Approved Supervisor. He has taught family therapy courses for over 20 years, written 10 family therapy books, and co-edited two books on therapy with couples.

The Basics Series

The Basics is a highly successful series of accessible guidebooks which provide an overview of the fundamental principles of a subject area in a jargon-free and undaunting format.

Intended for students approaching a subject for the first time, the books both introduce the essentials of a subject and provide an ideal springboard for further study. With over 50 titles spanning subjects from artificial intelligence (AI) to women's studies, *The Basics* are an ideal starting point for students seeking to understand a subject area.

Each text comes with recommendations for further study and gradually introduces the complexities and nuances within a subject.

DRAMATURGY
Anne M. Hamilton and Walter Byongsok Chon

HINDUISM
Neelima Shukla-Bhatt

RELIGION IN AMERICA 2E
Michael Pasquier

FINANCE (FOURTH EDITION)
Erik Banks

FAMILY THERAPY
Michael D. Reiter

For a full list of titles in this series, please visit www.routledge.com/The-Basics/book-series/B

FAMILY THERAPY

THE BASICS

Michael D. Reiter

NEW YORK AND LONDON

Designed cover image: © Getty Images

First published 2023
by Routledge
605 Third Avenue, New York, NY 10158

and by Routledge
4 Park Square, Milton Park, Abingdon, Oxon, OX14 4RN

Routledge is an imprint of the Taylor & Francis Group, an informa business

Library of Congress Cataloging-in-Publication Data
Names: Reiter, Michael D., author.
Title: Family therapy : the basics / Michael D. Reiter.
Description: New York, NY : Routledge, 2023. |
Series: The basics | Includes bibliographical references and index. |
Identifiers: LCCN 2022052759 (print) | LCCN 2022052760 (ebook) |
ISBN 9781032319780 (paperback) | ISBN 9781032320472 (hardback) |
ISBN 9781003312536 (ebook)
Subjects: LCSH: Family psychotherapy–Textbooks.
Classification: LCC RC488.5 .R455 2023 (print) |
LCC RC488.5 (ebook) | DDC 616.89/156–dc23/eng/20230111
LC record available at https://lccn.loc.gov/2022052759
LC ebook record available at https://lccn.loc.gov/2022052760

ISBN: 978-1-032-32047-2 (hbk)
ISBN: 978-1-032-31978-0 (pbk)
ISBN: 978-1-003-31253-6 (ebk)

DOI: 10.4324/9781003312536

Typeset in Bembo
by Newgen Publishing UK

This book is dedicated to my children Maya and Koji who will be the next generation in whatever field they choose to enter.

CONTENTS

ABOUT THE AUTHOR

Dr. Michael D. Reiter, LMFT, has been a practicing family therapist for the past 30 years. He earned his M.S. and Ed.S. in Counselor Education from the University of Florida with specializations in Marriage and Family Therapy and Mental Health Counseling. He then earned his Ph.D. in Family Therapy from Nova Southeastern University. Michael is a licensed marriage and family therapist in the state of Florida and an Approved Supervisor through the American Association of Marriage and Family Therapy.

Over his career, Michael has worked in home-based family therapy programs, community mental health centers, and in private practice. For the past 23 years, he was a faculty member at Nova Southeastern University teaching in the Division of Social and Behavioral Sciences, Clinical Psychology, Mental Health Counseling, and most recently in the Department of Family Therapy. He has been fortunate to gain training from some of the visionaries of our field including Insoo Kim Berg, Steve de Shazer, and Michael White. For 10 years Michael worked closely with Dr. Salvador Minuchin, founder of Structural Family Therapy, engaging in a training program for family therapy students. This endeavor culminated in the publication of Minuchin's last book, *The Craft of Family Therapy*, written by Minuchin, Reiter, and Borda. That book is in its second edition.

Michael has been heavily engaged in scholarship, having written 10 books, including *Therapeutic Interviewing* (2nd ed. Routledge, 2022), *Systems Theories for Psychotherapists* (Routledge, 2019), *Family Therapy: An Introduction to Process, Practice, & Theory* (Routledge, 2018), and *Case Conceptualization in Family Therapy* (Pearson, 2014). His books have been translated into Spanish, Polish, Chinese, Italian, and Korean. Michael has also published over 20 journal articles and presented at state, national, and international conferences regarding a variety of therapeutic interventions and family therapy models.

CONTRIBUTOR BIOGRAPHIES

Dr. Joshua L. Boe is an assistant professor in the Department of Couple and Family Therapy at Nova Southeastern University. Dr. Boe's clinical and supervision areas of interest include the training of narrative ethics and incorporating social justice into clinical and supervision practice. Dr. Boe's overarching research agenda focuses on promoting transgender inclusive healthcare and training transgender inclusive healthcare providers.

Dr. John K. Miller is the Director of the Sino-American Family Therapy Institute (SAFTI) and has been in clinical practice for over 30 years. He is a former full professor in both the USA and China, and a *US Fulbright Senior Research Scholar to China* (2009–2010). The SAFTI promotes international scholarly exchange opportunities between Eastern and Western students, scholars and clinicians.

PREFACE

30 years ago, I began my journey to becoming a family therapist. I had a lot of good teachers and was able to work with a few of the founders and leaders of our field. Over 20 years ago I became a teacher of family therapy. I feel fortunate that I am able, in this book, to introduce you to this field that has helped hundreds of thousands of families and millions of people around the world. Family therapy is an extremely life-changing phenomenon for clients and therapists.

As a Professor of Family Therapy, I have learned how to conceptualize and present ideas in ways that students can first understand and then, more importantly, implement. I hope that I've been able to at least do the first part for you in this book. I know this is only an introduction to the field, this is why this book is part of The Basics series. My hope is that you become as excited about the field as I, my colleagues, and my students.

I want to thank Dr. Joshua Boe and Dr. John Miller for their contributions to Chapters 10 and 11 respectively. Also, to all my students who provided you a little glimpse into a student's experience of learning and practicing family therapy. This was a chance for them to give back a little to the next generation (hopefully which you will become) of family therapists. They are Vanessa Bibliowicz, Defne Kabas Bici, Sienna deLisser, Joseph Alvaro Guerrero, Luis Guererro, Nailin Morera, Georgiann Neil, Elvan Okaygun, Kaitlin Osborne, Kayleigh Sabo, and Alana Tokayer. Shout out to Rosey Nguyen and Maya Reiter who reviewed a draft of the book and provided me with feedback. I want to thank Sarah Gore, from Routledge, who reached out to me about this book's viability and helped me see this project come to fruition. To everyone else at Routledge, who helped along in the process, thank you.

Each chapter is designed to orient you to the content material. There are several boxes in each chapter: Major Players, Fun Facts, and From a Student's Perspective. The Major Players box introduces you to one or more significant figures in the history of family therapy. The Fun Facts box provides you with more detail about one area of the content. From a Student's Perspective allows you a small window into one of my master's or doctoral students and their experience related to the chapter content. Every chapter ends with a bulleted summary and a glossary of important terms is provided, to help you glean the overall intent of each chapter.

Welcome to your introduction to the field of family therapy.

HISTORY OF FAMILY THERAPY

ORIENTING QUESTIONS

- What components led to the development of the field of family therapy?
- How is family therapy different than other types of counseling and therapy?
- What are some of the main reasons that people go for family therapy?

Congratulations! You are interested in the field of family therapy. Perhaps you want to learn more about it, or find out if this is a potential career for you; or perhaps this book has been assigned to you in a class. Whatever the reason you are reading this book, you are in for an amazing journey. Family therapy is a wonderful field. It is extremely important for healthy functioning, since family therapists guide individuals, couples, and families through difficult points in their lives and help them interact with others in ways that are more harmonious and supportive.

A HISTORY OF FAMILY THERAPY

Early History

Before we get into what family therapists do, let's discuss how we got to this point in the first place. On the first day of class for my master's students in the family therapy program at the university where I teach, I ask them three questions:

DOI: 10.4324/9781003312536-1

1. What year did formal psychotherapy begin?
2. What year did family therapy begin?
3. Why is there a gap between the two? (So, that's a hint that #2 is more recent than #1.)

Take a minute and try to answer each of these questions. Try to pick a specific year for #1 and #2.

My students give many different responses on when formal psychotherapy began—usually ranging all over the place, but typically somewhere in the 1900s. Then one student will come to the realization that the year must be related to Sigmund Freud. They then guess the early 1900s. We then discuss how the mid-1890s might mark the formal start of psychotherapy. However, the term "psychotherapy" had been used for several decades before this, particularly in relation to hypnosis and the alleviation of patients' symptoms. Freud had learned about hypnosis and used it in his early work; however, he also advanced many new ideas that came to be termed "psychoanalysis." His approach was known as "the talking cure." So, we have arrived at approximately 1895 as the start of psychotherapy. Let's move on to the start of family therapy.

When asked about this, my students are all over the map. They might suggest the 1920s, 1940s, or 1970s. While there is no specific year, I tend to think of 1956—the year one of one of the most important articles in family therapy history, "Towards a Theory of Schizophrenia," was published. However, there were precursors to this paper, such as a 1942 study by the American Association of Marriage Counselors—which eventually became the **American Association of Marriage and Family Therapy** (AAMFT), the most important association for family therapists in North America. The child guidance movement, spearheaded by Alfred Adler, also helped introduce many of the notions of therapy that were foundational for the field.

So, if we take 1895 as the start of psychotherapy and 1956 as the start of family therapy, we are looking at a 60-year gap between the two. Why was this so long? One primary reason was Freud, who singlehandedly did more for psychotherapy than anyone else. But at the same time, more than anyone else, he also held the field back. In a nutshell, Freud liked things his way and didn't like people going against him. Thus, there was little appetite for challenging his ideas or testing out new ideas. Further, one of his views is that a therapist does not meet with a patient's family members. This dictum did not promote working with multiple people at once.

Also remember that in the early part of the 20th century, we did not have many different psychotherapy theories. Psychoanalysis (the model that Freud developed) was the primary model for most of the 20th century. However, in the 120 years since its inception, psychotherapy models have expanded and proliferated. Let's play one more guessing game. How many different distinct models of psychotherapy are there today (including individual, couple, family, and group therapies)? Many students know that it is not one! They may guess 10, 20, or even 30. But they usually are not even close.

There are over 400 models of psychotherapy, and about 30 models of family therapy. But early in the history of psychotherapy, there were only a handful of different models. So those people who devotedly followed Freud would not meet with the parents, spouses, siblings, or children of their patients. Thus, those who did were challenging the establishment. And perhaps that is a good way to view the history of family therapy: as developed by people who were challengers to the status quo.

During the early part of the 20th century, psychotherapy was much more of a European endeavor, with Vienna, Austria being a hub of activity and growth. Freud, Freudians, and neo-Freudians began to have a diaspora, transporting these early ideas to many corners of the globe. Frankl, Jung, and Adler took Freud's initial ideas and built on them, developing their own theories of therapy. **Alfred Adler** played a crucial role in oiling the wheels of the family therapy movement. His approach, known as "individual psychology" or "Adlerian therapy," incorporated a larger view of the family and interpersonal connection. Further, Adler played a key role in the child guidance movement, which viewed children within the context of their families.

Major Players

Alfred Adler (1870–1937) was an Austrian medical doctor who was one of the initial members of the Wednesday Society, an informal discussion group that would meet at Sigmund Freud's house to discuss aspects of the newly emerging psychoanalytic approach. Adler eventually left and developed his brand of psychotherapy, called "individual psychology" (now referred to as "Adlerian therapy"). Adler's approach focused on issues of inferiority, and how the individual developed their way of understanding life through their family constellation and birth order. He was a proponent of parent education and influenced the child guidance movement. Adler was born into a Jewish family but converted to Christianity. However, in the 1930s, the Nazis began closing his Austrian clinics. This led Adler to immigrate to the United States for the last few years of his life. His legacy has held strong in individual, couples, and family therapy. You can even attend Adler University in Chicago, Illinois. This university was founded in 1952 by Rudolf Dreikurs, one of Adler's primary mentees. Adler was one of the first psychotherapists to utilize family therapy and Adlerian family therapy is still used today to help families improve their communication and connection with one another.

A second aspect that hindered the development of family therapy was the social view of problems. In the early part of the 20th century (and the latter part as well, but luckily not to the same degree), people did not go to therapists like they do today. If someone received psychological treatment, it tended to be in an institution for a serious issue, such as schizophrenia, hysteria, or neuroses. There was a severe stigma for people in needing and receiving psychological treatment. Family members were embarrassed when one of their own needed psychological help. They were often sent away to an insane asylum and received severe treatment, such as heavy medication, shock therapy, and sometimes lobotomies.

These are a few of the factors that limited the development of family therapy. So, what were some events that set the stage for family therapy to emerge as a field? By the end of World War II, families were severely traumatized. The extended separation put a strain on families. They worried that their loved ones might not make it back alive. Many didn't. Those servicemen who did come back from combat suffered serious psychological difficulties. Having been placed in a horrifying situation, they were no longer competent individuals and were having negative experiences. Society realized that individuals and families needed help. This led to Congress passing the National Mental Health Act of 1946. During the 1940s, various therapists started to work with families, but usually as a one-time assessment to help an individual client. The 1950s saw a more formalized way of working with families emerge.

Conjoint Therapy

What tends to make family therapy different than most other mental health professions is the desire and ability to work with multiple people at the same time. Early in the field's history, this was called **conjoint therapy**. Today, we just use the phrase **family therapy**. One question might be: what makes up a family? We tend to distinguish between the nuclear family and the family of origin. The **nuclear family** is the smaller subsystem and includes partners/spouses and any children they may have. For instance, my nuclear family consists of myself, my wife, and my two children. The **family of origin** is the family that the adults in the nuclear family come from. Thus, in my nuclear family, there are two families of origin: mine and my wife's. My family of origin includes my parents and my siblings. My parents each came from a family of origin; and if we continue this process, you will soon see that we are quickly talking about hundreds of people involved in a "family."

When family therapists talk about working with a family, they are usually referring to the nuclear family. However, this is not always the case. Sometimes it will be an adult and their parent, a couple and their in-laws (or "out-laws" as my ex-brother-in-law used to say), cousins, or other configurations. Later in the book, when we get into the various models, we will explore how they each may focus on different configurations. Some family therapists explore the multiple generations in a family more, while others primarily work with the nuclear family.

Schizophrenia's Influence

Perhaps it will be interesting for you to know that the birth of family therapy is related to schizophrenia. During the 1950s, when the field was in its infancy, many of the originators were working with people diagnosed with schizophrenia. Various psychiatrists were exploring schizophrenia from a wider view. For instance, **Frieda Fromm-Reichman** discussed the notion of the schizophrenogenic mother: a mother who is rejecting and overprotective, which leads the child (usually a young adult male) to become distrustful and resentful of others and display schizophrenic symptoms. **Theodore Lidz**, a psychiatrist, proposed the very related concept of schizophrenogenic parents. Lidz believed that there was an environmental cause of schizophrenia (and other mental illnesses). He proposed the concepts of **marital schism** (where there was overt conflict between parents that led to child dysfunction) and **marital skew** (where spouses seemed to be harmonious).

In 1956, the article "Towards a Theory of Schizophrenia" was published. In this article, Gregory Bateson and colleagues hypothesized that schizophrenia is not an internal mental disorder but rather a communicational disorder. This group received a grant to study the communication of schizophrenic individuals. They observed hospitalized schizophrenics interacting with family members (primarily their mothers). They identified a process where there was a confusion of messages—what they called a **double bind**—where the verbal message was about closeness while the nonverbal message pushed the other person away. The context also didn't provide space for people to talk about these paradoxical messages. This talking about the talk is known as **metacommunication**.

The Bateson Group were not the only therapists to enter family therapy through their attempts to work with people diagnosed with schizophrenia. Others, such as Ivan Boszormenyi-Nagy and Murray Bowen, developed their models based on trying to help schizophrenic individuals and realized the significant impact that families have on the functioning of schizophrenics.

Development of Theoretical Models

During the late 1960s and 1970s, family therapy models proliferated. The foundational models developed during this period are still the primary models in the field (with a few additions we'll look at in a minute). These include Mental Research Institute (MRI) brief therapy, Satir's Growth Model, Bowen Theory, strategic family therapy, structural family therapy, symbolic-experiential family therapy, and contextual therapy.

One of the interesting aspects of this nascent period of the field is how the founders interacted with one another. Given that the founders were learning on the fly, they began talking with and learning from one another. For instance, Salvador Minuchin traveled to Palo Alto, California to observe what was happening at the MRI. He saw them using a one-way mirror and installed one in the Wyltwick School, where he was working. He also met Jay Haley and recruited him a few years later to join him at the Philadelphia Child Guidance Clinic. For 10 years, Minuchin and Haley commuted to work together, exchanging theoretical ideas. Their two different theories (structural and strategic therapy respectively) were influenced by each other, and for a time people called them "structural-strategic family therapy."

Family therapy institutes were developed, and this is where people were trained. It was not like today, when you go to a university and earn a master's or doctoral degree in family therapy. These types of programs were not around then. The founders also utilized technology and audio and video recorded many of their sessions, sometimes seeing the same client so that people watching the videotapes could compare how they worked similarly and differently from one another.

The Influence of Postmodernism

In the 1980s and 1990s, the field of family therapy was influenced by postmodernism.

Modernism, in a simplified explanation, is the notion that there is a truth to things and that we can know that truth. In essence, modernism holds that there is a way that families should be, and therapists should work to change families so they fit this ideal. By contrast, **postmodernism** holds that there is no absolute truth. Utilizing notions from constructivism and social constructionism, the expertise in the therapy room began to shift from the therapist to the client. That is, therapists adopted a **not-knowing stance**, where the client is an expert on their meanings and the therapist is an expert on having a conversation that brings those meanings to the forefront. Several models of family therapy were developed that hinged their philosophical foundations on postmodernism, including collaborative language systems, solution-focused brief therapy, and narrative therapy.

One aspect that makes family therapy unique from all other psychotherapies is its openness to bringing multiple people and therapists into the therapy room. Besides having many family members present at the same time, family therapy utilizes co-therapists perhaps more than other fields. Further, since its inception, family therapy has attempted to unveil what occurs in the therapy room. One of the primary methods of doing this initially was through the one-way mirror, where one or more therapists met with the family in the therapy room while a group of family therapists watched and talked about what was happening from behind a one-way mirror.

This was taken even further through the reflecting team, which was developed by Tom Andersen in Norway. In a **reflecting team**, a group of therapists watch a therapist work with a family, usually from behind a one-way mirror. These two systems—the therapeutic system, and the reflecting team system—are autonomous: they do not tell each other what to talk about. However, they potentially impact one another. The reflecting team listens to the therapeutic conversation, and after a certain point in time—usually 30 to 40 minutes—the two systems change places. The reflecting team goes into the therapy room and the therapist and client go behind the one-way mirror. The members of the reflecting team then discuss aspects of the therapeutic conversation they were drawn to. Once they are finished, perhaps after 10 to 15 minutes, the two groups switch back to their original places. Then the therapist interviews the family about their reactions to what the reflecting team talked about.

The 21st Century

Over the last 20 years or so, family therapy has become more mainstream, with the privileges afforded to most other mental health professions (e.g., Baker Act privileges or serving on insurance panels). While the previous 30 years saw the proliferation of different models of family therapy, the 2000s focused more on the common factors of therapy that transcend all models.

Family therapy has tried to expand the notion of the system that it works with. Most people think that family therapists only work with families, but this is not the case. Using a "systems view" or a "relational perspective" allows family therapists to work with a wide range of clientele. This is because, over the last few decades, we have embraced a **biopsychosocial perspective** (see Figure 1.1). We are not the only field to do so; but this lets us see where problems are housed and whom they influence.

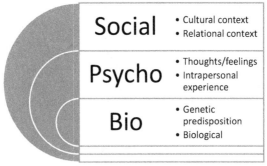

Figure 1.1 Family therapists have begun utilizing a biopsychosocial perspective.

Family therapists have also expanded their understanding of the terms that have defined the field, such as "marriage," "marital," "couple," and "family." This is because the field has attempted to become more inclusive, highlighting the importance of relational connections that go beyond the traditional heterosexual couple and biological children. We will focus more on family therapy's appreciation of diversity in Chapter 10. For now, we can talk about how, in this current century, family therapists view themselves as allies to the variety of family formations that exist.

Further, 21st century family therapy relies more on research (see Chapter 11). Larger-scale studies that show the effectiveness of models for particular types of clients with particular types of problems have become a core component of the family therapy field.

MAJOR PLAYERS

The history of family therapy features a variety of intriguing professionals who found their way into the field. I have included a "Major Players" section in most chapters to quickly introduce you to the founders of family therapy. In later chapters, we will explore in greater depth the ideas of the theories they developed. I present here their names so that you can start to get familiar with them:

Gregory Bateson	Insoo Kim Berg	Luigi Boscolo	Ivan Boszormenyi-Nagy
Murray Bowen	Gianfranco Cecchin	David Epston	Milton H. Erickson
Jay Haley	Don Jackson	Cloé Madanes	Salvador Minuchin
Mara Selvini Palazzoli	Guiliana Prata	Virginia Satir	Steve de Shazer
Paul Watzlawick	John Weakland	Carl Whitaker	Michael White

These are the major players in family therapy. They sit in the Family Therapy Hall of Fame. However, the field has had thousands of influential figures that we won't be able to recognize here.

Fun Facts

The field of family therapy is growing. In the United States, there are currently more than 125,000 family therapists. In the last 10 years, the field grew by almost 20%. The average age of family therapists is 43, with approximately 75% being female and 25% being male. Approximately 75% are White, 10% Hispanic/Latino, and 8% African American. The starting salary is about $40,000 and the average salary is just over $50,000. However, if you work in private practice in an affluent area with cash-paying clients, you can make over $100,000 a year. There are well over 100 graduate programs where you can get a degree in family therapy. To gain a better sense of the various marriage and family therapist (MFT) license requirements based upon the state as well as links to various MFT programs, visit mft-license.com.

DISTINCTION BETWEEN FAMILY THERAPY AND OTHER MENTAL HEALTH PROFESSIONS

Why have you decided to learn about family therapy? What about the other helping professions? What are the major differences between them? All the various helping professions do the same thing: we help people who are having some type of problem or symptom. However, we do so differently, often looking for different reasons why people are having problems and what we can do to help them.

There are various fields in the helping professions, including family therapists, marriage counselors, psychologists, psychiatrists, mental health counselors, social workers, addiction therapists, etc. While these distinctions might be based on one's graduate education or license, there is overlap. Any of these helping professionals can conduct family therapy sessions. So, what makes family therapists unique? Primarily it is how we view the theory of problem formation—that is, why people have problems in the first place. While I will be generalizing and simplifying here, family therapists tend to see problems as contextual and interpersonal, whereas most of the other professions view problem formation as being internal to the individual. We will explore this more in subsequent chapters; but for now, we can say that family therapists believe one person's difficulties are based on the rules of interaction between them and another person(s) based on the situation and type of relationship that they have. Don't be concerned if this doesn't fully make sense yet; it will by the end of this book.

So, what can family therapists do or not do that other professionals can or cannot? Family therapists do not have the rights to techniques or legal abilities that others do not. However, we do have a set of skills and ways of conceptualizing within our therapeutic tool pouch that most other therapists do not. We will cover this in Chapter 4. While psychologists and counselors can work with families, family therapists are likely to have been trained to much greater degrees in how to work with more than one person in the room at the same time.

If every therapist, regardless of type, can conduct family therapy sessions, what can't family therapists do that others can? Primarily, two things. First, there are various types of psychological testing that we are not trained to do, such as achievement, aptitude, and neuropsychological tests. The administration of these comes under the purview of clinical psychologists. Second, we cannot prescribe medications. That ability is given to psychiatrists (and in very rare circumstances to clinical psychologists). As a family therapist, if you believe one of your clients is having neurological issues or potentially needs medication, you should refer them to the appropriate mental health professional.

SCHOOLING

To become a family therapist, you will need to earn at least a master's degree. There are over 100 different MFT programs in the United States alone. Choosing one may be difficult; however, they mostly have the same curriculum (the courses you will need to take). Thus, your choice might be based on the location of the school, whether the school provides classes in person or online, and how much the program will cost. You should also consider whether the program is accredited (i.e., whether there is an overarching organization that sets certain standards for best practices that the program follows). All MFT programs will include courses that focus on ethics, human development, theories (particular models), psychopathology, and cultural diversity.

Most master's programs are around 60 graduate hours, with each course being three credit hours. This results in approximately 20 courses you will take. Almost all the courses cover the knowledge areas you will need for licensure. You will likely also have the opportunity to take a couple of elective courses so that you can focus and specialize. While you do not have to have a doctoral degree to become a family therapist, some people do for various reasons.

One of the most important of these is because the person wants to become a faculty member at a university and teach others about family therapy. There are two types of doctoral degrees that family therapists can get: a Ph.D., which is more of a research degree; and a DMFT, which is more of a clinical degree. There are also a few family therapists who get a Psy.D., which is a doctoral degree in clinical psychology, but who qualify by taking enough of the family therapy coursework, completing the needed clinical hours, and passing the family therapy licensure exam.

From a student's perspective

Thanks to a lot of therapy myself, I'd settled on an idea I *thought* I was comfortable with: I would simply never love my job, but I'd build a rich life in other ways. I spent four idyllic college years studying comparative literature—a major that barely translates into abundant career prospects. So, I spent seven years making the desired realities of CEOs come true as an executive assistant. I'd had enough. Thanks to the delightful synchronicity of life, I had the opportunity to radically change careers. My very last boss asked me what my dream role at the company would be, to which I replied, "The guidance counselor." That was my eureka moment. In many ways, the equivalent of an adult guidance counselor is an MFT. Plus, all of my favorite therapists were MFTs; and once I realized this was my path, it was their ranks I wanted to join. Also, once you get a taste of systemic thinking, it's very hard to go back.

Sienna deLisser, master's therapist

LICENSURE

Family therapy is a regulated field. Just like a doctor, lawyer, or real estate agent must have certain education and pass a test, family therapists must do so as well. In the United States, each state has its own requirements for **licensure**, which will include specific areas of education (you will complete this in your master's family therapy program); work experience (which you will complete partly during your graduate education and for about two years after graduating); supervision experience (you will need to be supervised by a credentialed supervisor for all the sessions you have before you are licensed—but don't worry, they won't have to be in the room with you when you are providing therapy services); and competency (you will need to pass a national test). To maintain your license, you will need to stay in good standing (pay a fee every two years and not have complaints against you), as well as earn a certain amount of **continuing education units** (through workshops and training).

Family therapists also will need to have **liability insurance**, as there is always the possibility that a client (or a client's family) will sue them for malpractice. While this is rare, there are family therapists (like there are doctors, lawyers, car mechanics, teachers, and cooks) who don't always do the best job. George Carlin, who was the world's greatest comedian (if you haven't heard of him or seen him, do yourself a favor and watch him on YouTube), once said that somewhere in the world is the world's worst doctor. And someone has an appointment with them tomorrow. The same can be said of family therapists. Therefore, the field is regulated. You need to have the necessary education, the necessary clinical training, the necessary direct client contact hours, the necessary supervision, and the necessary guidelines (see Chapter 2 for an explanation of ethics). This takes years and years of focus in this field so that you will be competent, effective, and ethical. With all of these components, the field of family therapy attempts to produce professional, qualified, ethical, and effective therapists.

PROFESSIONAL ASSOCIATIONS

Family therapists are overseen by one of several different **professional associations**—where members get together to talk about best practices, develop ethical guidelines, and network with one another. They usually hold at least one conference per year where members attend various workshops so they can learn about new developments and techniques. Our field believes in lifelong learning, since family therapists are continuously trying to better understand family processes and the best ways to work with them.

In the United States, the primary professional association for family therapists is the AAMFT. Worldwide, there is the International Family Therapy Association and the International Association of Marriage and Family Counselors. There are also professional associations in various regions of the world, such as the Asian Academy of Family Therapy. Family therapists do not have to belong to any of these organizations; however, most do. Membership requires payment of an annual fee, which usually provides you with member benefits, such as discounts to attend conferences or a subscription to a journal that might be associated with the organization.

WHY FAMILIES SEEK OUT FAMILY THERAPISTS

There are as many reasons that people go to a family therapist as there are people. Further, it is not only families that prefer working with family therapists: individuals and couples do as well. This is because of the perspective that family therapists take, where they are looking at the problem in context rather than just in relation to a single person.

For families that come to therapy, they do so usually because of some type of problem that is impacting more than one person in the family. This could involve issues of divorce, remarriage, depression, psychological disorder, drug abuse, depression, school problems, or normal parent-child difficulties.

On average, clients come for about seven therapy sessions. These sessions usually last about one hour. Depending on the model of family therapy used (we will cover a variety of these in some of the later chapters), one, two, three, or more members of the family will attend the sessions. The cost of sessions is dependent on whether the family is going through their insurance (and how many sessions they get and what the co-pay is); whether this is an agency (which a lot of new family therapists work in while they are earning their supervised hours for licensure); or whether this is private practice (which will usually cost the most and likely have a more experienced therapist providing services). The cost can range from free (most likely at a non-profit social service agency) to several hundred dollars per session (usually in private practice). The cost is also likely to go up or down based on locale, with areas frequented by high socioeconomic communities being more expensive than areas with primarily lower socioeconomic communities.

GLOSSARY

- **Biopsychosocial perspective**: The view that people are impacted on multiple layers, including the biological, psychological, and social.
- **Conjoint therapy**: Working with more than one person in a family at the same time in a session.

- **Double bind**: Where a person is punished regardless of how they respond to a situation.
- **Family of origin**: The family in which a person was born and raised.
- **Family therapy**: The mental health profession that works with families to help them change their behavior patterns.
- **Licensure**: The granting of a license that demonstrates a person's knowledge and competence in a profession.
- **Marital schism**: When spouses overtly fight with each other, which leads to the child having psychological or behavioral problems.
- **Marital skew**: When one spouse seems to be functioning well and the other does not, which leads to the child having psychological or behavioral problems.
- **Metacommunication**: Communication about one's communication.
- **Modernism**: The idea that there is a reality that we can know.
- **Not-knowing**: A philosophical stance where the therapist doesn't presume to know how the client makes sense of their own experience.
- **Nuclear family**: The family that one lives in, usually consisting of the parents and children.
- **Postmodernism**: The idea that there is no reality, but that we construct reality based on socially agreeing on what is.
- **Professional association**: A group of people in a field who network together to discuss the best practices and ethical guidelines for that profession.
- **Reflecting team**: A group of therapists who watch a family session and then discuss what they watched as the family observes them.

CHAPTER SUMMARY

- Family therapy was primarily developed in the 1950s.
- Family therapy focuses on the family as a unit.
- The history of family therapy was born out of work with schizophrenics.
- The 1960s and 1970s saw a proliferation of many different models of family therapy.
- The latter part of the 20th century saw an increased focus on the notion of postmodernism, where family therapists moved away from absolute truth.

- Family therapists engage in many of the same activities as other helping professions, yet their view of the problem focuses more on what happens between people rather than within a person.
- Family therapy is a regulated field. Family therapists must be licensed and need education, supervision, and clinical hours to become licensed.

REFERENCE

Bateson, G., Jackson, D. D., Haley, J., & Weakland, J. (1956). Toward a theory of schizophrenia. *Behavioral Sciences, 1*, 251–264.

2

FAMILY THERAPY ETHICS

ORIENTING QUESTIONS

- What are the core ethical principles that family therapists use when they engage clients?
- How do family therapists react when a client is suicidal?
- What are the unique ethical issues that family therapists must tackle that individual therapists do not?

How do you decide how to be with people? Do you follow the Golden Rule—do onto others as you would have them do unto you? The Silver Rule—don't treat people in a way you would not want to be treated? What do you base your morals and values on? You are likely not to think too much about the rules of interaction that are in place when you are with friends or family. However, your actions are informed by certain guidelines, whether they be religiously or humanly based.

Family therapy, like all fields of psychotherapy, is based on a set of professional standards that defines how to be (and not to be) with clients. We call these standards **ethics**. These are different from **laws**, which are rules of governance overseen by a government body. You are beholden to both, meaning you should be ethical and lawful. Each mental health field has its own ethical codes that it follows; however, these codes have many more similarities than differences. This chapter presents the primary ethical concepts that apply when working with families. It discusses specific ethical codes from the American Association of Marriage and Family Therapists (AAMFT) and the International Association of Marriage and Family Counselors

DOI: 10.4324/9781003312536-2

(IAMFC), so you can get a sense of how they are worded and the specific expectations of therapists' conduct.

CORE ETHICAL PRINCIPLES

Ethical principles were developed to ensure clients are treated respectfully and professionally. They guide therapists' actions, keep therapists accountable, and are a way for the field to demonstrate professionalism to society. In this section, I outline the primary ethical principles (see Figure 2.1). These principles form the mindset of therapists and become the standards of behavior that therapists should utilize when working with clients. If a client ever tried to sue a therapist, one of the components that would exonerate the therapist is how closely they adhered to these standards of practice.

Beneficence

Family therapy was developed to help people. This is the primary aim of all therapies—to do good. The ethical principle associated with this idea is **beneficence**, which means there is some type of benefit the client gets from their interaction with the therapist. Family therapists utilize all their skills to try to help clients make positive changes. All the techniques that family therapists learn and practice are designed to help clients shift from their current state so they meet their therapeutic goals.

This notion of doing good and helping the client move forward is so important that if the therapist believes what they are doing is not helping the client, they should end the therapeutic relationship. However, you cannot just abandon your client, as that may negatively impact them. If family therapists believe they are no longer being useful to the client, then there is a conversation to be had and a plan to be made on how to move forward: either changing what is happening in therapy, changing therapists, or discontinuing therapy.

> **AAMFT Code of Ethics:**
>
> 1.9: Relationship to Client
>
> *Marriage and family therapists continue therapeutic relationships only so long as it is reasonably clear that clients are benefiting from the relationship.*

IAMFC Code of Ethics:

Couple and family counselors withdraw from a counseling relationship if the continuation of the relationship is not in the best interests of the client or would result in a violation of ethical standards.

Nonmaleficence

While beneficence is about doing good, **nonmaleficence** is about not doing bad. This is similar to the Hippocratic Oath that many in the medical professions take: "First, do no harm." Therapists should not harm or take advantage of the client. This means that you don't exploit the client. You should always be aware of the impact therapy is having on the client and check in with them if you think some aspect of therapy is having a negative impact on their life.

This principle implies that family therapists must be competent. You should not engage in practices that you are not trained in. Family therapists learn their skills through classroom teaching, workshops, training, and reading books written by other therapists. At some point, they will try out a new technique for the first time. Before doing so, they should have thought about the implications and perhaps talked with colleagues and/or a supervisor to ensure they are utilizing that technique in the appropriate manner.

AAMFT Code of Ethics:

1.11 Non-Abandonment

Marriage and family therapists do not abandon or neglect clients in treatment without making reasonable arrangements for the continuation of treatment.

IAMFC Code of Ethics:

Couple and family counselors do not harass, exploit, coerce, or manipulate clients for personal gain.

Autonomy

Some people think they can bring in a family member whom they think is out of control or behaving badly and the therapist will be able to force them to act differently. This is not the role of the therapist and is unethical. Family therapists respect people's **autonomy**: their right to make their own decision. Therapists will almost always try to get clients to choose what they want to do in their lives. One of the only exceptions to this is when the client is at risk of harming themselves or someone else. In that case, the therapist is obligated to warn the authorities so that the client and others are safe. Over the last several decades, the legal system has increased its utilization of therapy as a part of court rulings. Therapists should respect a person's decision whether to engage in therapy while also being upfront about the consequences of not engaging in therapy (i.e., that the therapist will send a letter to the court explaining the person's participation—or not—in the therapeutic process).

AAMFT Code of Ethics:

1.8 Client Autonomy in Decision Making

Marriage and family therapists respect the rights of clients to make decisions and help them to understand the consequences of these decisions. Therapists clearly advise clients that clients have the responsibility to make decisions regarding relationships such as cohabitation, marriage, divorce, separation, reconciliation, custody, and visitation.

IAMFC Code of Ethics:

Couple and family counselors promote client autonomy and facilitate problem solving skills to prevent future problems. They do not make decisions for families or family members when the decision-making rightfully belongs to the family and/or family members. When it is beneficial, couple and family counselors share clinical impressions and recommendations for the purpose of better informing families.

Perhaps the first way that family therapists enact the principle of autonomy is through **informed consent**. Therapy is a contractual relationship, and informed consent sets the guidelines for the relationship. Before starting therapy, the client should read and sign the informed consent form, which stipulates, in clear and understandable language, the nature of the services the therapist will offer. In family therapy, all individuals aged 18 and older must sign the informed consent form. Parents (or legal guardians) must also sign consent for minors. For the most part, people under 18 cannot sign consent, but they can sign **assent**—that they agree to treatment.

AAMFT Code of Ethics:

1.2 Informed Consent

Marriage and family therapists obtain appropriate informed consent to therapy or related procedures and use language that is reasonably understandable to clients. When persons, due to age or mental status, are legally incapable of giving informed consent, marriage and family therapists obtain informed permission from a legally authorized person, if such substitute consent is legally permissible. The content of informed consent may vary depending upon the client and treatment plan; however, informed consent generally necessitates that the client: (a) has the capacity to consent; (b) has been adequately informed of significant information concerning treatment processes and procedures; (c) has been adequately informed of potential risks and benefits of treatments for which generally recognized standards do not yet exist; (d) has freely and without undue influence expressed consent; and (e) has provided consent that is appropriately documented.

IAMFC Code of Ethics:

Couple and family counselors inform clients of the goals of counseling.

Confidentiality

The therapist-client relationship is sacred. Because clients are likely to be vulnerable and will be discussing painful, embarrassing, and often frightening thoughts and experiences, they need to feel secure and safe to do so. Thus, therapists observe the principle of **confidentiality**—that they will not tell anyone else what they are told in session. Similar to the Las Vegas slogan, "What happens in Vegas stays in Vegas," what happens in the therapy room stays in the therapy room. You cannot go home and tell your partner or your friend who said what in session. Further, if you are ever out in public and you see your client, you cannot make any gesture or communication to the person. This is because it would put them and you in a position of potentially having to explain to someone else how you know that person. If the client comes up to you, yes, you can talk to them; but you should try to keep things very informal and brief, not getting into any therapeutic material.

While confidentiality is one of the hallmarks of psychotherapy, there are times when the therapist can or must break confidentiality. Therapists can talk to others about what a client has said if the client has agreed and signed a release of information. Otherwise, therapists can break confidentiality if required by law. This happens when talk in a session leads to a suspicion that there has been abuse of a child, a person with a disability, or an elder. Therapists must also break confidentiality if the client is in immediate danger of harming themselves or another; or if there is a court order.

AAMFT Code of Ethics:

2.1 Disclosing Limits of Confidentiality

Marriage and family therapists disclose to clients and other interested parties at the outset of services the nature of confidentiality and possible limitations of the client's right to confidentiality. Therapists review with clients the circumstances where confidential information may be requested and where disclosure of confidential information may be legally required. Circumstances may necessitate repeated disclosures.

IAMFC Code of Ethics:

Each person who is legally competent and deemed an "adult" must be provided a confidentiality agreement with the couple and family counselor(s). The agreement must be time limited, consistent with legal statutes. The parameters of confidentiality must be agreed upon by the client and counselor.

JUSTICE

Over the last 20 years, the notion of justice has become more prominent in the psychotherapy arena. **Justice** in this context means that therapists provide services to all people regardless of age, disability, ethnicity, gender, gender identity, health status, national origin, relationship status, religion, sexual orientation, or socioeconomic status. Thus, therapists should engage in non-discrimination. You cannot decide not to work with someone because of any of these components. However, you might tend to specialize, where you work primarily with teens, LGBTQIA+ individuals, or couples. Many therapists do specialize, such as working with families dealing with eating disorders; so it is important to have a good referral network to help families get connected to a therapist who might best help them.

AAMFT Code of Ethics:

1.1 Non-Discrimination

Marriage and family therapists provide professional assistance to persons without discrimination on the basis of race, age, ethnicity, socioeconomic status, disability, gender, health status, religion, national origin, sexual orientation, gender identity or relationship status.

IAMFC Code of Ethics:

Couple and family counselors must monitor their places of employment and make recommendations to promote cultural awareness, inclusivity, and human growth and development.

Recently, family therapists have begun talking about **social justice**—ensuring there is fairness in who can receive treatment. Not all people are treated the same: marginalized populations have had more difficulty accessing therapy services. Further, there may be differences economically in who can access different services. Social justice practices explore how therapists can provide appropriate services to all potential clients. This may involve providing pro-bono (free) sessions to clients who cannot afford to pay or perhaps working on a sliding fee scale so that people pay based on their income.

Major Players

Lynn Hoffman (1924–2017) was one of the most influential family therapists. She earned an undergraduate degree in English literature from Radcliffe College, and a master's in social work from the Adelphi School of Social Work, specializing in family therapy. Hoffman was an advisory editor to the two most important family therapy journals: *Journal of Marital & Family Therapy* and *Family Process*. She was a faculty member at the Ackerman Institute and promoted the early systems theory (see Chapter 3) that was the foundation of family therapy; she then advocated for the postmodern and collaborative approaches that were prominent around the turn of the 21st century. Her most famous book was *Foundations of Family Therapy*, in which she presented many of the cybernetic ideas (see Chapter 3), as well as an overview of many theories of family therapy.

Fidelity

The therapy relationship is based on trust. This relates to the ethical principle of **fidelity**—where therapists act in ways to ensure the client believes in the therapy relationship and process. By following the ethical guidelines and always being professional, therapists send a message to clients of their competence, concern, and integrity.

Part of this trustworthy relationship is that the therapist will not take advantage of the client. One of the primary ways of ensuring this is not having a dual relationship with the client. **Dual relationships** are when the therapist and client have two distinct roles. We know one role is the therapy-client relationship. The other could be friend-friend, family member-family member, or business owner-customer. This is one of the reasons that therapists can never do therapy with a family member. As part of this idea, therapists are not allowed to engage in any type of sexual relationship with their clients (and some ethical codes hold that a client is a client for life, whether they continue coming to sessions or not). While there are times when you cannot always prevent dual relationships, for the most part, you should never work therapeutically when you know the client in another context.

AAMFT Code of Ethics:

1.3 Multiple Relationships

Marriage and family therapists are aware of their influential positions with respect to clients, and they avoid exploiting the trust and dependency of such persons. Therapists, therefore, make every effort to avoid conditions and multiple relationships with clients that could impair professional judgment or increase the risk of exploitation. Such relationships include, but are not limited to, business or close personal relationships with a client or the client's immediate family. When the risk of impairment or exploitation exists due to conditions or multiple roles, therapists document the appropriate precautions taken.

IAMFC Code of Ethics:

Couple and family counselors inform clients in writing of their counseling qualifications, costs of services, goals of counseling and reasonable expectations for outcomes.

Veracity

As you just read, therapists should enhance the level of trust in the therapy relationship. Another way to do this is by following the ethical principle of *veracity*—being truthful. Family therapists should be clear and honest when interacting with clients. What you say to clients should be accurate, clear, and consistent.

AAMFT Code of Ethics:

8.4 Truthful Representation of Services

Marriage and family therapists represent facts truthfully to clients, third-party payors, and supervisees regarding services rendered.

IAMFC Code of Ethics:

Couple and family counselors maintain accurate and up-to-date records.

Beneficence	• Do Good
Nonmaleficence	• Do No Harm
Autonomy	• Self-Determination
Justice	• Fairness
Fidelity	• Trustworthiness
Veracity	• Truthfulness

Figure 2.1   Family therapists try to uphold the general ethical principles that guide our code of conduct with clients.

SUICIDALITY

The ethical principles of beneficence and confidentiality come into greater focus when a client is potentially suicidal. This situation is perhaps one of the most fear-inducing for a therapist, as you have a responsibility to try to prevent the client's suicide. However, you cannot control someone else. What you can do is try to help them move past their desire to harm themselves and toward a life they want to live.

Let's take a few minutes to define many of the terms relating to suicidality. **Suicidal ideation** is having thoughts about suicide. Most people think about suicide at some point in their lives. This isn't problematic. However, it is a warning sign that therapists need to be aware of so that they can explore this situation more deeply. **Suicidal intent** is when the person has a goal of killing themselves. The greater the level of suicidal intent, the greater the risk that the person will engage in self-harming behaviors. A **suicide threat** is a communication from the person, whether verbal or nonverbal, that they may make a suicide attempt soon. The threat could be overt—"I am going to go home today, go into the bathtub, slice my wrists, and wait to die"; or more covert— "I don't want to feel this excruciating pain anymore and would do anything to get rid of it." A **suicide plan** outlines how the person would attempt to complete suicide. This may be by taking an overdose of pills, hanging themselves, or shooting themselves with a gun. The risk of completion is higher when people have access to the means (i.e., they have a gun or have the pills). Lastly, a **suicide attempt** is the action the person takes in trying to kill themselves. These concepts are usually progressive, in that the person first has the idea, then the desire, then the means; and then engages in the action (see Figure 2.2).

Figure 2.2 People usually go through a progression of actions around suicidality.

Family therapists should always be aware of the possibility of suicidality. Some believe that you should do a suicide assessment with every single client, regardless of the presenting problem. If a therapist doesn't do so, they open themselves up to possible litigation if their client completes suicide and they did not take appropriate actions—including an assessment of suicidality.

Once a family therapist knows there is suicidal intent, they have a **duty to protect** their client. It is their responsibility to try to ensure the client's safety. This may involve breaking confidentiality and bringing in law enforcement to temporarily hospitalize the client until they are no longer actively suicidal. If self-harming is not imminent, the therapist should develop a **safety plan**, which focuses on the various resources available to the client so they can be more aware of what to do when they are having suicidal thoughts.

DUTY TO WARN

While therapists have a duty to protect, they also have a **duty to warn**, which means they must break confidentiality if they believe their client is likely to harm someone else. This responsibility was born from the *Tarasoff v. Board of Regents of the University of California* court ruling. A university student had informed his therapist that he wanted to kill another student, whom he specified by name. The therapist was concerned and contacted campus police, who found the client to be rational and took no further action. No one informed the potential victim. The client eventually did kill her. Her parents then sued a variety of individuals and the university. From this ruling, therapists have a duty to warn someone if there is imminent danger and the intended victim is identifiable.

ETHICS SPECIFIC TO FAMILY THERAPY

What have been presented thus far are the ethical principles and responsibilities of all mental health professionals (although they might be worded a bit differently based on which ethical code is being used). This section discusses ethics that are specific to family therapists. These include multiconfidentiality, equity, secrets, and diagnosis.

Multiconfidentiality

When working with an individual, you need only maintain confidentiality for one person: the client. However, as more people enter the therapy room, their confidentiality must also be held. While everyone in the room is viewed as "the client," confidentiality is afforded to every individual in the family that comes to the session. It doesn't matter how many people are in the room—the therapist must not tell anyone outside of the session what was talked about.

However, things get a little more complicated when the family therapist works with various subsystems. Let's say you are working with a family of five people: a husband, wife, and three children. There are times when you want to work with everyone; but at other times, you will want to work with a subset of the larger family—perhaps just the parents, just the children, the father and daughter, or maybe just an individual. The issue here is that you will have to be clear with everyone about whether what is talked about in those sessions is fair game to be discussed with other members of the family.

If, during the previous session, the therapist had met with just the children, could they divulge what was talked about when meeting with the full family in the next session? On the one hand, yes, if all the children are minors, since parents have a right to know what is happening in their children's treatment. On the other hand, no, as the children may have spoken based on an expectation that what was said would remain confidential. This issue goes back to the ethical principle of fidelity, or trustworthiness. The way to address this is for the family therapist to be very transparent at the beginning when separating people in sessions. They could approach this in one of two ways:

- "We are going to be meeting individually for one session. I just want to be clear that I do not believe in family secrets. Given this, whatever we talk about in that session will be fair game to be brought up when we reconvene everyone."
- "We are going to be meeting individually for one session. I explained to you all about confidentiality. That will hold for those meetings as well. I won't bring up with everyone what we talk about individually."

Either approach is acceptable; but the therapist should be very overt and clear from the get-go about which position they are going to take. This provides the client with enough information to be autonomous and make informed choices.

Fun Facts

While you cannot 100% guarantee that a client (or a client's family) won't report you to the licensing board or try to sue you, following all the ethical principles to the best of your ability can reduce that risk. The following are a few of the most common reasons why clients report or sue family therapists:

- excessive self-disclosure;
- boundary issues;
- improper training; or
- inadequate note taking.

While self-disclosure is a therapeutic technique and is very important for joining (for further details please see Chapter 4), the question is who the self-disclosure is for. If you disclose something because you think it will help the client, great. However, if you are disclosing for your own purposes (e.g., to make yourself feel better or more important), then you should keep it to yourself.

The main boundary issue that gets therapists in trouble is having or attempting to have some type of sexual relationship with a client. While there are some ethical codes that say it might be okay to engage in a relationship with a client after a significant amount of time has passed since you last saw them (usually around two years), most ethical codes say that a client is a client in perpetuity—meaning they are your client for life.

We talked in Chapter 1 about therapists continuously learning. When you do so, you expand your therapeutic tool pouch. However, there are times therapists try techniques that they haven't been trained and supervised on. When these techniques go wrong, therapists open themselves up to liability if they have not been properly trained.

Lastly, your therapy case notes are your documentation of what happened in therapy. They should be detailed enough that they explain what happened each time you met with the client (or even talked to them on the phone or via technology). The rule of thumb in therapy is that if it is not documented, it did not happen. If you didn't

document something (especially something like a suicide assessment), you open yourself up to possible negative consequences.
Thus, family therapists should document every decision they make
regarding the appropriate treatment for a client.

Secrets

In individual therapy, the client is likely to tell the therapist many
secrets. The therapist is not obliged to divulge those secrets to anyone
(except in those very limited circumstances covered by the guidelines on breaking confidentiality). However, in family therapy, this
becomes a much murkier issue. If you meet with one member of the
family, they may tell you something that makes a significant difference to your work with other members of the family. The question
is then: what to do about this?

You might think to yourself: "Why would someone meet separately with family members? Isn't meeting the whole family together
what makes family therapy unique?" Yes; however, there are times
when you may want to meet individually, and it is in this context that
the issue of secrets arises. There may be things that a person would
not say in front of family members but would when they are alone.
For example, these might relate to domestic violence, affairs, child
sexual abuse, drug use, or a desire to divorce or end a relationship. If
you only met with the full family, these extremely important topics
might never surface. However, when they do, you will then need to
decide what to do with the secret.

As described previously in the discussion on multiconfidentiality,
you should be upfront with clients on how you will handle meeting
separately with family members. You do not want to become triangulated between family members where you are holding a secret
from one over the other. This will likely lead to a sense of betrayal
for one family member when they eventually realize that you knew
information that would have been important for them to know too.

Equity

Equity means that you consider the wellbeing of all your clients. In
family therapy, the family is considered your client, and the family is
composed of multiple people. You should not treat one person better
than another. There are times when you might join one person and

support their position over another, such as in a domestic violence situation; but just because you are taking this stance does not mean that you are valuing one person more than another.

Carl Rogers—perhaps the most influential psychotherapist of all time—promoted the notion of **unconditional positive regard**, which is caring about an individual as a human being who, if given the right conditions, can strive for growth. You should have unconditional positive regard for all your clients. This doesn't mean you must like everything that they do. Clients will do a lot of things you do not agree with (e.g., treating people poorly, shoplifting, or smoking cigarettes) or even approve of (e.g., engaging in domestic violence, dealing drugs, or engaging in infidelity). This doesn't mean that you treat them worse for it. All people deserve respect. They need to be treated equally well by you, although you may use different techniques with each to help them move toward their goals.

Besides thinking about the welfare of the family members in your office, you must also think about all the people that will be impacted by the interventions happening in therapy. This notion is called **multidirected partiality**. Your client is connected to many other people in a web of relationships; when your client changes, their interactions with others will change, which will impact those people's interactions with others.

DIAGNOSIS

The bulk of psychotherapists attempt to understand the symptoms that people experience through the lens of diagnostic assessment. One of the most commonly utilized tools in this process is the *Diagnostic and Statistical Manual*, which is currently in its fifth edition. This book contains all the psychological disorders that most people think about when they think of psychologists trying to explain what is wrong with a person. These include bipolar disorder, schizophrenia, major depressive disorder, and dissociative identity disorder, to name a few. Insurance companies usually require one (or more) diagnoses to be identified for reimbursement.

Given this, what does a family therapist do when working with multiple people? As we will see over the course of the next few chapters, family therapists view the etiology of people's symptoms as not being internal to them, but rather as interpersonally based. Families come to therapy with an **identified patient**: a person that they say is the problem and that needs to be fixed. This is likely the person in the family that is exhibiting symptoms. If the family therapist diagnoses the person, this may send a message to the other family members that the family's problems are the fault of that person. This may lead them to feel absolved of behavior that in fact is maintaining the problem.

Many family therapists have stopped diagnosing, as they do not want to perpetuate the belief that the identified patient is the problem. However, this can be problematic if the family is paying for services through their insurance company, which will likely require a diagnosis to reimburse. Ethically, therapists cannot "up-code" a diagnosis, where they make a diagnosis that may not be accurate but that they know is reimbursable. Any time you diagnose a client, it must be accurate. This is serious business, as it is entered in the client's official record and may have a serious impact on their life. This goes to the ethical principle of veracity.

From a Student's Perspective

I have a love/hate relationship with ethics. I love it because it is so important – ethics is meant to protect the therapist and client, and it maintains the integrity of our profession. But it scares me too. It can be complex, overwhelming, and hard to decipher—and with dire consequences (as a former lawyer, I know this all too well). There's a lot of gray: in some situations, the ethical path is easy; and in others, it can be hard to know what to do. Or sometimes the situation seems easy in theory, but in practice we may feel reluctant to take the ethical path—to listen to that nagging voice inside our heads saying, "This doesn't feel right." What I've come to learn is that ethics is not something that should be feared, but should actually make us feel safe. Okay, so perhaps I have a mostly love/drop of hate relationship with ethics.

Alana Tokayer, master's student

ETHICAL DECISION MAKING

As you can see throughout this chapter, there are many fundamental principles and guidelines that family therapists must follow to ensure they are practicing soundly and with the client's best interests in mind. These ethical codes are not always black and white. Therapists are always in the process of making ethical decisions. While most therapists try to be ethical, there are times when a decision is not that clear. When this happens, therapists go through an ethical decision-making process to try to determine the best course of action. The more that therapists rest their decisions on these ethical principles, the more they protect themselves, the client, the field, and society.

GLOSSARY

- **Assent**: When people under 18 years old agree to engage in therapy.
- **Autonomy**: People making their own decisions.
- **Beneficence**: Doing good.
- **Confidentiality**: Keeping private what was said in the therapy session.
- **Dual relationships**: Having more than one role with a person (e.g., being someone's therapist as well as their business partner).
- **Duty to protect**: The therapist's responsibility to try to prevent a person from harming themselves.
- **Duty to warn**: The therapist's responsibility to try to prevent a client from harming someone else.
- **Ethics**: Principles that govern people's behaviors.
- **Fidelity**: Being loyal and truthful in one's relationships.
- **Identified patient**: The symptomatic person that the family presents as being the problem in the family.
- **Informed consent**: Giving people enough information about the therapeutic process for them to knowingly choose to engage in therapy.
- **Justice**: Servicing all people, regardless of their situation.
- **Laws**: Rules of governance, usually set by a governing body.
- **Nonmaleficence**: Not doing bad; not harming another person.
- **Safety plan**: A plan that focuses on the actions a client can take to prevent them from making a suicide attempt.
- **Social justice**: Focusing on issues of justice in wider society.
- **Suicidal ideation**: Having thoughts about suicide.
- **Suicidal intent**: Wanting to kill oneself.
- **Suicide attempt**: The action of trying to kill oneself.
- **Suicide plan**: Devising a means of killing oneself.
- **Suicide threat**: Expressing the desire to kill oneself.
- **Unconditional positive regard**: Caring about a person as a human being, regardless of other factors.
- **Veracity**: Being truthful to another person.

CHAPTER SUMMARY

- Family therapists must follow both ethical principles and local laws.
- The core ethical principles are designed to ensure therapists are helping people and not harming them.
- Family therapists must ensure that clients are willingly choosing to engage in therapy and hold almost everything they say in confidence.
- Family therapists must do whatever they can to ensure that clients do not harm themselves or someone else.
- All therapists follow ethical principles, and family therapists also have several additional ethical issues that they need to deal with.

3

SYSTEMS THEORY

ORIENTING QUESTIONS

- What is a system and why is it so important for family therapists?
- How does a systems perspective help family therapists conceptualize why a family is having problems and what interventions to use to help them?
- What are the primary patterns of interaction that families engage in?

WHAT ARE SYSTEMS?

You are extremely familiar with systems; you just might not have been using this term when describing them. When you were born, you were born in and into many systems. If you were born in a hospital, you were born in a hospital system. You were also born into a family system, which was part of a larger family system, which was part of an even larger family system, etc. You were born in a country that had political, legal, educational, and cultural systems. Your family likely had a connection to a religious system. As you can see, you are part of many systems, and these systems interconnect with one another.

So, what is a system? A **system** is a group of interacting parts that function as a whole. Your refrigerator is a system with doors, lights, motor, coolant, ice maker, etc. that function as one unit. Your car is a system with an engine, wheels, body, frame, and gasoline (or electric battery) that need each other to work properly. *You* are a system with interacting parts such as the heart, brain, blood, lungs, stomach, etc.

DOI: 10.4324/9781003312536-3

that all function as one. In family therapy, the primary system that we look at is the family. The family has individual components (each family member) that have a unique way of relating to one another. This way of relating makes it *that* family and not another family.

The other prominent system we explore in family therapy is the **therapeutic system**. The family that you are working with is not the same family they are at home. By you being there with them, they are different, if just a little. You influence them and they influence you. So, just keep in mind that you are never seeing the whole picture. Therapy is about partiality.

Yet family therapists like to talk about *wholes*. We like to work with the *whole* family. We like to get the *whole* picture. In session, we want to hear the *whole* story. While we will never get there, we use the word "whole" as if it really is. On a related note, one of family therapy's most important statements is: "The whole is greater than the sum of its parts." What does this saying really mean?

Bear with me a moment while we do a little math (and don't worry, this will be the only math in the whole book). From a systems view, see if you can solve the following equation: $1 + 1 = 3$. How does this equation make sense?

My children, from when they were just a few years old, knew that $1 + 1 = 2$, not 3. So, how did family therapists learn to do incorrect math? When I ask my graduate students this question on their first day in the program, they have a few interesting answers. Someone will invariably say that there is a husband and wife, and together they make a baby, which is three. Others guess that it is two families that come together to make a third family. While these are fine guesses, they are not quite accurate. So, let's solve the equation.

We can do a couple of substitutions of words for numbers. By swapping Person for 1, our equation becomes Person + Person = 3. What is that 3? It is the *relationship* between the people. Think of your relationship with the person you are closest to. It has not been like that for the whole of the relationship. There were times you were farther apart or closer. The 3 stands for the qualitative rather than quantitative aspect of the relationship. And it is that quality that family therapists are most interested in. Let's do just a little more math to understand this better (we are still working on the same equation, just making it a little more complex).

In a two-person system, there is only one relationship, between the two people. What happens if they have a child? There are now three people. What would the equation be? $1 + 1 + 1 =?$. The answer is

7. A four-person family would be: 1 + 1 + 1 + 1 = 14. And a five-person family, like the one I grew up in, would be 1 + 1 + 1 + 1 + 1 = 30. How did this happen? Let's substitute letters for numbers and here is what we get:

- Individual Person: A; B; C; D; E (5 total)
- Two-person relationships: A + B; A + C; A + D; A + E; B + C; B + D; B + E; C + D; C + E; D + E (10 total)
- Three-person relationships: A + B + C; A + B + D; A + B + E; A + C + D; A + C + E; A + D + E; B + C + D; B + C + E; B + D + E; C + D + E (10 total)
- Four-person relationships: A + B + C + D; A + B + C + E; A + C + D + E; B + C + D + E (4 total)
- Five-person relationship: A + B + C + D + E (1 total)

If you add up all these different components, we get 30.

Okay, I know this might be a little confusing, so let's get a little more personal so you can better understand 1 + 1 = 3. If you are like me, you may have an ex about whom you say to yourself, "Who would be more stupid than me to have dated this person, because they were awful?" When you think about why the relationship ended, it is likely because the other person was controlling, mean, lazy, or a cheater. But here is a little secret: that is not why the relationship ended. Yes, the other person was bad. But the relationship ended because there was one person who was controlling in the relationship to someone that didn't want to be controlled. Or someone who was lazy in the relationship to someone that wanted to move forward and strive. Or someone who cheated on someone that didn't want to be cheated on.

After your relationship ended with this person, you might have found out they were dating someone else and the two of them were quite happy. How could this be? It is because we substituted you as one of the 1s in our equation and put in someone else. Maybe that person was okay with their partner having a wandering eye. Or they wanted to be controlled. They were not the same 1 as you and thus, the quality of that relationship changed.

Hopefully, you will see that this explanation has been partial. We are only talking about the people in a particular family. But those people interact with other individuals and systems outside of the family. In other words, the individual is a subsystem of the family; the family is a subsystem of the family of origin; and the family of origin is a subsystem of the wider society. This can be seen quite nicely in Uri Bronfenbrenner's **ecological systems theory** (see Figure 3.1). He held that the individual is just one part of many systems (Bronfenbrenner & Morris, 2006). The **microsystem** contains those systems that have direct contact with the person. These include nuclear family members, friends, teachers, work colleagues, etc. The individual not only is impacted by these systems, but can also impact them. The **mesosystem** is where the systems the individual is connected to interact with one another—for instance, your partner interacts with your work colleague, or your parent interacts with your friend. The **exosystem** encompasses the formal and informal social structures that impact one or more of the microsystems, such as extended family or the work setting. The largest system, the **macrosystem**, displays how cultural elements impact the person. These include socioeconomic status, ethnicity, laws and rules, and the social condition.

Take a second and think about the various systems you are housed in. One thing you'll hopefully recognize is that this picture is not static. There may have been people in your microsystem 10 years ago that are no longer there. Or you may have belonged to a religious institution but stopped attending many years ago. To help us understand this, there is one more system to keep in mind: the **chronosystem**. "Chrono" refers to time and the chronosystem focuses on normal life transitions that people go through that include human development processes, family lifecycle changes, and historical events.

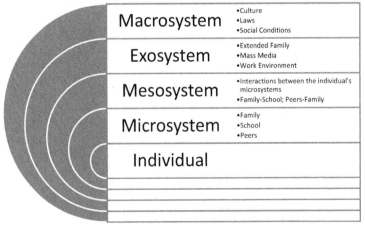

Macrosystem	•Culture •Laws •Social Conditions
Exosystem	•Extended Family •Mass Media •Work Environment
Mesosystem	•Interactions between the individual's microsystems •Family-School; Peers-Family
Microsystem	•Family •School •Peers
Individual	

Figure 3.1 Bronfenbrenner's ecological systems theory.

CHANGE

This leads to another famous family therapy saying: "Change in one part of the system will change the system." With our equation, we substituted you out for another person; but let's keep you and the other person in the equation. Let's have you be one of the 1s and your current partner or someone you are close to be the other 1. Right now, it is a good relationship. How could we make it bad? (We wouldn't do this, since you learned in Chapter 2 about nonmaleficence; but for the sake of learning the concept, just go with me.) Think about what you could do to ruin your relationship. I'm sure you could come up with many ideas, some funny and some mean. But by you changing, you change the interaction and thus change the relationship.

This happens in families as well. Families can be viewed like a child's mobile. It maybe has five objects (e.g., elephants, birds, or balls) hanging on it. If you made one of those components heavier, all the other components would have to change their positions. In families, think of what happens when one member becomes an addict. Their dysfunctional behavior has a ripple effect throughout the rest of the family. How does this happen?

UNDERSTANDING PATTERNS

Relationships maintain themselves because they are **patterned**— that is, there are repetitive ways that people behave with one another. If you live with someone, think about how things will go when you (or they) get home tonight. You are likely to be able to predict what it will look like. This is because there are rules to your interactions. Does the person tend to ask you about your day? Or will they avoid and ignore you? And you know when there is something wrong in the relationship—they are acting differently. That is, they are not engaging in the behaviors that are typical of your relationship.

Major Players

Gregory Bateson (1904–1980) was a famous anthropologist who explored the notion of cybernetics—how systems are self-regulating. He was a core member of the Macy Conferences, which brought people together from a variety of fields to study cybernetics. Bateson applied cybernetic concepts to human (and animal) relationships. He received several grants to study communication and brought on board Jay Haley, John Weakland, and Paul Watzlawick. When studying schizophrenic communication, Bateson hired Don Jackson. Jackson was the only psychiatrist in the group. While Bateson never became a therapist, his concepts of systems, homeostasis, information, and cybernetics became foundational components for many of the early models of family therapy. Bateson's most famous book was *Steps to an Ecology of Mind*.

Family therapy, and really all therapy, is about pattern interruption. The question is: what pattern are you trying to interrupt? Some people try to interrupt patterned thinking, or patterned reinforcement contingencies, or patterned understanding of self. Family therapists interrupt patterned interpersonal interactions. There are three main types of patterned relationships: symmetrical, complementary, and parallel.

Have you ever found yourself doing the same thing with someone where maybe you are both yelling at each other, each showing love to the other, or each ignoring the other? If so, you've experienced a symmetrical relationship. **Symmetrical relationships** occur when both individuals engage in the same behavior. There are two types: competitive and submissive. **Competitive symmetrical relationships** happen when both people try to one-up each other. This occurs when you and someone else are in an argument. Your voices are likely to get louder; you are likely to try to make your point the more they try to make theirs; and unfortunately, the more they insult you, the more you insult them. **Submissive symmetrical relationships** occur when both people try to defer to each other. Have you ever agreed with someone to do something on Saturday and the conversation goes something like this:

You: What do you want to do?
Other: I don't know. What do you want to do?
You: I don't know. You choose.
Other: No, you choose.

Competitive and submissive symmetrical relationships demonstrate that people move in the same direction as one another.

Complementary relationships occur when the more one person does, the less the other does. In family therapy, we have a famous scenario we call the **pursuer–distancer relationship**. You might have played one, the other, or both roles at some point in your dating life (although the pattern happens in nonromantic relationships as well). In this relationship, the more one person pursues, the more the other distances. We can say this the other way—a term that we call **punctuation**: the more one distances, the more the other pursues.

The last type of pattern is a **parallel relationship**, in which there is a back-and-forth negotiation. Now, your relationship with a person doesn't only function by one of these. You use all of them, but it depends on the context of your interaction. For instance, with your partner, you might engage in a competitive symmetrical relationship when you are deciding what to do for fun; a submissive symmetrical relationship when deciding who is going to cook dinner; a complementary relationship around financial matters; and a parallel relationship about child rearing. Figure 3.2 presents a visual representation of

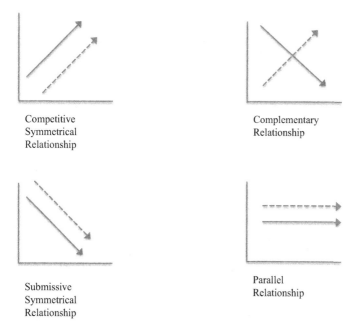

Competitive
Symmetrical
Relationship

Complementary
Relationship

Submissive
Symmetrical
Relationship

Parallel
Relationship

Figure 3.2   Relationships function based on established patterns.

these types of patterned relationships, where the solid line represents one person and the dotted line the other person.

So, which is the best pattern? The answer is, none and all. These patterns are neither good nor bad. They just are. It depends on what they are about. A competitive symmetrical relationship of showing love would seem to be good. However, it would be quite bad if it was about harming the other person. A complementary relationship can be good when both partners are doing or not doing what they like. Perhaps you like to cook, and your partner is an awful cook. What better than the more you cook, the less they do? However, it can be problematic when it is the more you earn for the family, the less they do. This may lead to a non-equal relationship and potential resentment.

Patterns are repetitive interactions and are based on overt and covert rules. **Overt rules** are those that are known to people. Perhaps in your family, it was stated, "We eat dinner together," "You must say 'Ma'am' or 'Sir'," or "Friday nights are family game nights." **Covert rules** are ways of being that are unspoken. No one ever told you, but you knew not to talk to dad when he had that look on his face; or you knew that if you didn't get the answer you wanted from mom, you could go to dad.

These overt and covert rules inform how people can be with one another, and are demonstrated in various patterned relationships. These rules might focus on two, three, or four-person interactions (or more, depending on how many people there are in the family). When we look at the family as a whole, we see that it functions in ways that maintain itself. That is, families develop a **homeostasis**, where they function in a steady state.

The word "homeostasis" has roots meaning "same state." While it may not be that common in popular culture, family therapy's history rests upon this notion. The thought is that families try to maintain their steady state—they try to keep their homeostasis. There is not one homeostasis for families. Each has its own. You've seen this when you've gone over to friends' houses when they've had their family there. Some families are quite loud. Others are quiet. Some are playful. Others are serious. Just like there is no good or bad pattern of relationship, there is no good or bad homeostasis. The question is: does this way of being work for the family at this point in time?

To help you understand the concept of homeostasis a bit better, think about your air conditioning (AC) unit. You set it at a certain level—let's say 70 degrees. It's summer and the sunlight shines through the windows and heats up the house. The AC unit has returns that take air in and gauge what temperature it is. When it is around 70 degrees, the AC unit stays off. However, when it gets above a certain temperature (let's say 73 degrees), the AC unit activates and puts out cold air until the temperature of the house is back to the status quo of 70 degrees.

When we talk about homeostasis, we are not talking about functional or dysfunctional (good or bad). Homeostasis is just the current dynamic of the family. You are probably comfortable in your family's current homeostasis and would be uncomfortable in a different family's way of being. If we go back to our AC example, you are comfortable at 70 degrees. If you go to someone's house that has their AC set at 65, you will probably be uncomfortably cold. If you go to someone's house that has their AC set at 75, you will probably be uncomfortably hot. However, if over time you slowly adjusted your AC from 70 to 70.1 to 70.2 and kept raising it by 0.1 degrees every few weeks, you would eventually find that you were comfortable at 75 degrees. So, just keep in mind: a family's homeostasis never stays the same. It changes over time.

We'll make this process a little more complicated here. The primary systems theory that has been the foundation of family therapy is called **cybernetics**, which is a focus on how systems are self-regulating. They do this through feedback. Systems utilize positive and negative feedback loops to help balance change and stability processes. **Positive feedback loops** are when information comes into the system that it is moving beyond the status quo; in essence, positive feedback focuses on **change** (see Figure 3.3). **Negative feedback loops** are when the system takes in information and enacts processes to maintain the status quo; in essence, they focus on **stability** (see Figure 3.4).

Just be careful to not think that the words "positive" and "negative" in this context are about good and bad. They just describe processes of whether there is a change or no change. Sometimes it is good that there is no change, such as when a family member who has started abusing drugs is encouraged to return to behaving well and thus prevent the family from falling into a crisis. Sometimes it is good that there is a change, such as when a family begins treating an adolescent as a young adult in preparation for launching them into adulthood.

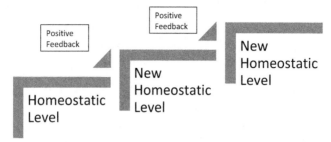

Figure 3.3 Positive feedback leads to change and a new homeostatic level.

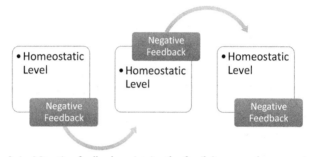

Figure 3.4 Negative feedback maintains the family's current homeostasis.

FAMILY LIFECYCLE

A family will experience many different homeostatic processes throughout the course of its lifecycle. This is because families need to change their functioning, and the rules of interaction, so they can handle the challenges at each lifecycle stage. Families, like individuals, go through a development process. A typical family starts with two adults who come together in the couple stage. They then have a child and must change and adapt so they can take care of the child. The family then expands when the child reaches school age, and the family must accommodate the school system. The child then becomes an adolescent, and the family must adapt once again to begin to give this member more freedom. At a certain point (usually around 18), the family will launch the child. Depending on how many children there are, the parents may become empty nesters. They then experience life without children and must reestablish their couplehood. This period has become a prime time for couples to separate or divorce. They then enter a time when they are likely to retire and must find

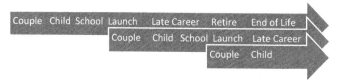

Figure 3.5 At any one time, there are likely three generations of a family at different stages of the family lifecycle.

meaning outside of their careers. Lastly, they become elderly and face end-of-life events.

While one nuclear family is going through the family lifecycle, there are other families that are doing so as well, but are at a different stage. When a couple launches a child, the child is starting a new family lifecycle. The couple is also a subsystem of their families of origin, where their parents are at a later life stage. Figure 3.5 presents a three-generational view of family lifecycle development.

While this may be the traditional path of families, there is a wide diversity of family formations. Some people choose never to have a partner or children. Others will divorce and potentially remarry. Others will never launch. Regardless, many family therapists think that families are more prone to have symptoms when they are shifting from one family lifecycle stage to another. This is because the homeostasis (the patterns and rules) that helped it to function and succeed in one stage is not useful in the next. The family did not adapt enough so that it could change its functioning. This is usually when they come to see you. So, how do you interrupt the problematic patterns families are having so they can engage in positive change?

Fun Facts

According to the most recent U.S. Census, less than 18% of American households are characterized by married parents with children—what we would call our traditional nuclear family. In 1970, this number was approximately 40% of U.S. households. Across the world, the number of individuals who are getting married and staying married has been consistently declining. People are getting married later in life, due to many factors, including the need for both individuals to gain education and employment. The median age for women to get married is now 27, while for men it is 29. In 1950, the average ages for women and men to get married were 20.3 and 22.9, respectively. This delay in marriage (if people get married at all) is also leading to people having children later in life, as well as fewer children than in previous generations. Currently, the average age to have children is 26 for first-time mothers and 31 for first-time fathers.

PATTERN INTERRUPTION

We have laid the foundation for how families maintain themselves through their patterned interactions. Unfortunately, families also maintain problematic patterns (what in the early years of family therapy were called "dysfunctional patterns"). The good news is that patterns are not inherent and immutable. They are developed over time, and they can change. Just think about a habit that you had in the past, such as nail biting or twirling a ring on your finger. The habit wasn't there from when you were born. Somehow it developed; and with effort, it changed.

There is also more good news. We do not need everyone in the family to try to change to enact change in the family. How many people do we need to meet with for family therapy to be successful? Just one! This is because, if you remember, a change in one part of the system can lead to systemwide change. Now, the more people in the family who attempt to change, the more possibilities there are that someone's change will be sufficient to change the patterned relationships and homeostasis of the family.

If we go back to our types of relationships, we can see that if there is a symmetrical relationship that is problematic, we would need to get one of the two (or both) to do something different. Instead of continuing to escalate like the other person, we would try to get the person to take a one-down position. In a complementary relationship, we would try to get one of the people to change their normal response—instead of doing less, maybe doing more. Take a second and think about a meaningful relationship you have with someone that is currently experiencing some difficulties. Try to figure out what the main pattern is in the relationship. What is your role in that pattern? Now, the next time you interact with the person and realize that the pattern is happening, act 180 degrees differently than you normally would. What happens when you do this? If this outcome is more desired than what you normally get, then continue with how you are engaging them. Eventually, this will become your new normal (your new homeostasis).

From a Student's Perspective

As a family therapist, I think about many relationships at the same time. It is difficult because I do not see one person but a whole family in the clinic. They all have their perspective on one issue, and they are all right! Every person/system has its own rules and when people come together, they create a new system that comes with even more rules. It is sometimes a struggle to consider everybody's needs, desires, and expectations at the same time. The way I go about it is to have them feel heard by each other. Sometimes that is all they wanted to achieve anyways.

Defne Kabas Bici, master's student

So, how do we actually interrupt these patterns? Is there a best way of doing so? The latter part of this book presents 10 different family therapy theories that have their own ways of pattern interruption. There is more good news here: there is not just one right way to help a family change. There are unlimited ways!

The systems concept that highlights this is called **equifinality**, which means that there are many paths to the same endpoint. Unfortunately, we sometimes hear people say, "This will only work out if my partner does X," or "I have tried everything." These are people who have a limited view of their options. We know they haven't tried everything because they haven't achieved their goal yet (although not every goal is achievable, people don't realize they always have more options than they think). As Salvador Minuchin used to say: "People are richer than they think they are." This is because there are more pathways available to them.

The thought example I like to use when talking about equifinality involves baseball. How many ways are there for an offensive player to get to first base? Take a few moments to try to brainstorm this ... Have you got the answer yet? Let me first show you what equifinality looks like in Figure 3.6.

Okay, so batter up! How many ways for the offensive player to get to first base? The answer is six:

Figure 3.6 Equifinality holds that there are multiple starting points to get to the same outcome.

- the batter hitting the ball and getting either a hit, an error, or fielder's choice;
- walking;
- being hit by a pitch;
- an uncaught third strike (with the batter running to first base before the ball is thrown there or they are tagged);
- a pinch runner; and
- catcher interference.

I think this is a good example to get you in the ballpark of understanding equifinality, because you probably thought there were only two or three ways. However, it is not the best example because there are a finite number of ways. In relationships and families, the pathways are exponential.

LINEAR VERSUS CIRCULAR VIEWPOINTS

Most psychotherapies operate from a straightforward **linear viewpoint**, where A leads to B. In many ways, most people around the world think in these terms: "If I do X, Y will happen." It is what the scientific method is based upon. Therefore, when a family comes to therapy and designates an identified patient, they expect you to do something about it. For instance, a family comes because their 12-year-old son is "acting out" by not doing what they are telling him to do. They believe if you do one of your psychological interventions, you will make the son change. The family is likely to be shocked when you take a different stance!

Families are likely to be using a linear viewpoint. They are wrong. They should be adopting a circular viewpoint, like the family therapist does. **Circular viewpoints** hold that parts of a system mutually influence each other. The son is impacted by the parents, who are also impacted by the son. Influence doesn't only flow one way; it is mutual and simultaneous (see Figure 3.7).

Circular viewpoints are important for family therapists as they help to keep the notion of context in the foreground. People's actions always occur within a context, and the context involves relationships. Think about where you work or where you go to school. There are rules for each of those contexts and, based on how your boss, teacher, colleague, or classmate acts toward you, you will act in some way toward them. But keep in mind the notion of punctuation. When they come to work or school, they are experiencing you and reacting to you. This is the chicken-egg dilemma. Are you acting toward them in a way based on how they acted toward you? Yes. But they are acting toward you based on how you have acted toward them. Perhaps a better way of visualizing this interaction is through a circular metaphor (see Figure 3.8).

As you can see, there is no start or stop point in this interaction. You are likely to pick one (probably the top middle "You act" circle),

Figure 3.7 A circular viewpoint holds that people simultaneously and mutually influence one another.

Figure 3.8 Punctuation holds that there is no start point in the circular interactions of people.

but that is an arbitrary start point. Also, remember the chronosystem. Relationships are predicated on time. Today's interaction does not happen outside the context of what happened in the relationship yesterday, last month, and last year. While people may say, "It is forgiven and forgotten," we might be able to forgive but we don't forget.

These are the basic concepts of systems theory, helping family therapists to see how family members are connected to one another. A problem doesn't just arise; it happens within a context of interactions that people put meaning to. Family therapists attempt to determine what that family's unique patterns are—its homeostasis—and then figure out how to engage in pattern interruption so that a new homeostasis occurs, which the family members prefer.

GLOSSARY

- **Bronfenbrenner's ecological systems theory**: There are multiple systems at play that mutually influence one another.
- **Chronosystem**: How systems change over time.
- **Circular viewpoint**: A perspective based on two (or more) things mutually influencing one another.
- **Competitive symmetrical relationship**: The more one person does a behavior, the more the other person does that behavior.
- **Complementary relationship**: The more one person does a behavior, the less the other person does that behavior.
- **Covert rules**: Rules that are unspoken and perhaps unconscious.
- **Cybernetics**: The theory of how systems maintain themselves through self-regulation.
- **Equifinality**: There are many pathways to the same end.
- **Exosystem**: The social structures that impact one or more microsystems.
- **Homeostasis**: When a system maintains a steady state.
- **Linear viewpoint**: Perspective based on one thing causing another thing.
- **Mesosystems**: Those systems that impact the individual when they interact with one another.
- **Macrosystem**: The influence that cultural elements have on people.
- **Microsystems**: Systems that impact the individual.
- **Negative feedback loop**: Information coming into a system to maintain its current homeostasis.

- **Overt rules**: Rules that are known to people.
- **Parallel relationship**: A back-and-forth of behaviors between people based on negotiation.
- **Pattern**: A repetitive way of behaving with one or more other people.
- **Positive feedback loop**: Information coming into a system that leads to change.
- **Punctuation**: The arbitrary start and stop points for an interaction.
- **Submissive symmetrical relationship**: The less one person does a behavior, the less the other person does that behavior.
- **Symmetrical relationship**: Both people do the same behavior.
- **System**: A group of interacting parts that function as a whole.
- **Therapeutic system**: Everyone involved in the psychotherapy process.

CHAPTER SUMMARY

- Family therapists attempt to understand how systems function— primarily the family system, as well as the therapeutic system.
- People engage one another through patterned behaviors and relationships.
- Family therapists believe that people engage in behaviors based on the rules of the context.
- Families tend to maintain a homeostasis—a way of being with one another—that is based on rules of interaction.
- Systems maintain homeostasis based on both stability and change.
- All therapies focus on pattern interruption, although they differ in what patterns they are trying to interrupt.
- Family therapy is predicated on circular causality rather than linear causality.

REFERENCES

Bateson, G. (1972). *Steps to an ecology of mind.* Ballantine.

Bronfenbrenner, U. & Morris, P. A. (2006). The bioecological model of human development. In W. Damon & R. M. Lerner (Eds.). *Handbook of child psychology* (pp. 993–1023). John Wiley & Sons.

CORE COMPETENCIES OF FAMILY THERAPISTS

ORIENTING QUESTIONS

- What are the primary core competencies that family therapists need so they can be effective in their jobs?
- How do family therapists focus on themselves, since they are the main therapeutic tool?
- What are the basic therapy skills that therapists use when working with clients?

Many people decide to become therapists because for much of their lives, people have been going to them when they've had troubles. You may have had similar experiences, where friends and family members have said that you're easy to talk to, that you give good advice, or that you should become a therapist. However, when these individuals start on a graduate training program, they find that it is not as easy as they thought. They learn that there are specific ways and techniques of interacting with clients, and that these ways are likely different than what they've been using to connect with friends and families.

Family therapy is a field that is predicated on the therapist being quite skillful as well as knowing the craft of family therapy. Both are aspects that must be learned. While there are some innate ways of being that can help in this process, these ways of being (what we call self-of-the-therapist) need to be honed and used properly. In this chapter, we describe some of the primary skills and competencies that family therapists must utilize to be effective.

DOI: 10.4324/9781003312536-4

CORE COMPETENCIES

Ethically, family therapists must be competent. The question then arises: what are they competent about? **Competency** means that the person can do something successfully. The American Association of Marriage and Family Therapy (AAMFT) developed a listing of core competencies for practitioners, including 128 competencies. They are organized around six primary domains:

- admission to treatment;
- clinical assessment and diagnosis;
- treatment planning and case management;
- therapeutic interventions;
- legal issues, ethics, and standards; and
- research and program evaluation.

There are also five secondary domains: conceptual; perceptual; executive; evaluative; and professional.

It is beyond the scope of this book to get into every AAMFT core competency. When you finish your master's program in family therapy, you should have covered each of these to one degree or another. Figure 4.1 provides a sampling of the various core competencies.

SELF-OF-THE-THERAPIST

While some people want to become a therapist because they have been the person friends and family seek out to talk to, others choose this field because they have had an experience in their past that was troubling, and they found therapy to be useful. There is an idea that some therapists are **wounded healers**. In either case, the therapist does not come into the therapy room as a blank slate. You are a person with a past, beliefs, values, primary ways of being (which we would call a personality), and biases. And how you engage in the room impacts the client and what happens in the therapeutic process.

Because of this, many training programs focus on the **self-of-the-therapist**. In the early years of psychotherapy, particularly for Freudian psychoanalysts, the therapist had to go through their own analysis. This was to prevent them from engaging the client based on

Domain 1: Admission to Treatment	
1.2.1 Perceptual	Recognize contextual and systemic dynamics (e.g., gender, age, socioeconomic status, culture/race/ethnicity, sexual orientation, spirituality, religion, larger systems, social context).
1.3.1 Executive	Gather and review intake information, giving balanced attention to individual, family, community, cultural, and contextual factors.
Domain 2: Clinical Assessment and Diagnosis	
2.1.4 Conceptual	Comprehend individual, marital, couple and family assessment instruments appropriate to presenting problem, practice setting, and cultural context.
2.4.2 Evaluative	Assess ability to view issues and therapeutic processes systemically.
Domain 3: Treatment Planning and Case Management	
3.3.1 Executive	Develop, with client input, measurable outcomes, treatment goals, treatment plans, and after-care plans with clients, utilizing a systemic perspective.
3.4.5 Professional	Monitor personal reactions to clients and treatment process, especially in terms of therapeutic behavior, relationship with clients, process for explaining procedures, and outcomes.
Domain 4: Therapeutic Interventions	
4.1.1 Conceptual	Comprehend a variety of individual and systemic therapeutic models and their application, including evidence-based therapies and culturally sensitive approaches.
4.5.1 Professional	Respect multiple perspectives (e.g., clients, team, supervisor, practitioners from other disciplines who are involved in the case).
Domain 5: Legal Issues, Ethics, and Standards	
5.2.1 Perceptual	Recognize situations in which ethics, laws, professional liability, and standards of practice apply.
5.4.2 Evaluative	Monitor attitudes, personal wellbeing, personal issues, and personal problems to ensure they do not impact the therapy process adversely or create vulnerability for misconduct.

Figure 4.1   Sample of the AAMFT core competencies.

Domain 6: Research and Program Evaluation	
6.1.1 Conceptual	Know the extant marriage and family therapy literature, research, and evidence-based practice.
6.3.4 Executive	Determine the effectiveness of clinical practice and techniques.

Figure 4.1   Continued

their own past issues. This is known as **countertransference**, which currently is used to describe when the therapist has a personal reaction to the client.

You want to make sure that the decisions you make in the therapy room are based on clinical appropriateness rather than your own issues. Thus, one of the main core competencies of family therapists is consistently reviewing your own biases to ensure they don't negatively impact what is happening in the session. This takes a lot of work and self-reflection. To this end, you should engage in **reflexivity**, where you assess your knowledge, values, beliefs, and attitudes to see how they are impacting you as a therapist.

There are times over your career as a family therapist (or any career) where you may experience the symptoms of **burnout**—being emotionally exhausted when exposed to stress over a long time. When becoming a family therapist, you will be working for six to eight hours per day with people who are in severe emotional pain, have experienced terrible trauma, are seriously conflictual with one another, and are anxious, depressed, and miserable. Many therapists may develop **compassion fatigue,** when they care so much about their clients that they internalize their clients' pain.

The risks of burnout and compassion fatigue are quite high for therapists. Thus, you will need to find ways to mitigate them. In our field, we talk a lot with clients about **self-care**: what they are doing to ensure they are emotionally and psychologically sound. This is also a needed skill for family therapists. **Therapist self-care** is extremely important so that therapists are functional and effective inside the therapy room, but also are living an enriching life when they don't have their therapist hat on.

There are lots of ways that you can engage in therapist self-care. You can talk with a supervisor or colleague about some of your struggles: exercise; go on vacation; ensure there are good boundaries between work and home life; avoid alcohol and drugs; hang out with people you like; meditate; have "me" time; and most of all, have fun. You should be consistently doing these things and not waiting until the point of experiencing burnout. At that point, it may be too late. Effective family therapists prioritize therapist self-care every week.

JOINING

In some professions, not much time is needed to develop a working alliance. Your exterminator or plumber doesn't spend more than a few moments making sure that you will be open and engaged. Therapists must do this as the therapeutic relationship is one of the most important factors for positive client change. In therapy, we call the connection between therapist and client the **therapeutic relationship**, or **therapeutic alliance**.

The way of developing the therapeutic relationship is through **joining**—the active process of connecting with clients. Joining is both a mindset and an event. You should always be thinking about how what you are doing with your clients will connect you. This is the mindset aspect. How you do this is the event aspect. From the first contact with clients, the therapist is joining. Perhaps this is over the phone or in the waiting room on the way back to the office. Joining can also be more formal, where you spend a portion of the first session asking clients to tell you about themselves. Even if you've never been in a therapy room before, you have engaged in this process of joining many times throughout your life. Think about the last person you met. You probably spent time feeling each other out, asking them questions about where they were born, where they went to school, what type of work they do, what music they like, etc. In lay terms, we call this "small talk." It is a way for people to begin to come together and make common cause.

Joining is an extremely important skill, since all the techniques the therapist uses are predicated on a strong working alliance. At some point during therapy, you will likely want to challenge your client. You will be better able to challenge when you have a strong connection. We can look at this as having money in the bank. Each connection you make is a deposit and each challenge is a withdrawal. If you challenge too much too soon, the client might take offense and possibly not come back.

All psychotherapies focus on the therapeutic relationship as it is a common factor in how clients change. Family therapists can find the skill of joining a bit more difficult, since we are not just joining one person, but several. Further, we are entering into an already charged family atmosphere and are trying to negotiate our way through this by making a connection to each person and not discounting anyone.

One way of doing this is by exhibiting **neutrality**, which is a position of accepting each person's understanding without taking it as truth. For instance, a family might come in saying, "Our daughter is out of control." If you turn to the daughter and say, "Scarlett, what's going on that you are so out of control?", you have already aligned with the parents and helped solidify her as the identified patient. She will likely view you as another adult whom she cannot trust. Instead, you could say something like, "Scarlett, your parents say that you are out of control. I don't know you. Can you tell me what you see going on?" Here, the therapist has remained neutral and begun to hear everyone's viewpoint. They are also making a covert statement that people will need to expand since there are multiple perspectives present.

Major Players

Scott Miller (1958-) received his bachelor's degree in psychology from Brigham Young University and a master's and Ph.D. in counseling psychology from the University of Utah. He worked for a time at the Brief Family Therapy Center in Milwaukee, Wisconsin, which was the birthplace of solution-focused brief therapy (see Chapter 9). He then co-directed and co-founded the Institute for the Study of Therapeutic Change and the International Center for Clinical Excellence. Miller's approach highlights the therapist's receptiveness to client feedback. His model is predicated on a strong therapeutic alliance and the use of client feedback. He developed the Outcome Rating Scale and the Session Rating Scale, which therapists give to clients so they can get the client's input into what is working in therapy. He has written many books, including *The Heroic Client: A Revolutionary Way to Improve Effectiveness through Client-Directed, Outcome-Informed Therapy* and *Better Results*.

UNDERSTANDING CLIENT MOTIVATION

Being able to hold multiple perspectives in the conversation at the same time is an extremely important skill for family therapists. One aspect of this is that, in a family, each individual likely has a different motivation level for change. While the family is a unit, the members that comprise it are unique individuals. Thus, family therapists need to keep in mind that not everyone will agree on what the problem is or what they want to see happen in therapy. Thus, one core competency is working with people in the room who are at differing levels of readiness for change.

One way of viewing readiness for change is through a five-stage process: precontemplation; contemplation; preparation; action; and maintenance (Prochaska et al., 2013). The **precontemplation stage** is when the person does not think there is a problem. This is the typical alcoholic who, when someone confronts them about their drinking, says, "No. I can handle my liquor." The person in the **contemplation stage** thinks there might be an issue, but are not ready to do anything about it yet. In the **preparation stage**, the person knows there is a problem and is setting the stage for change. Perhaps this is through finding a therapist, stopping hanging around troublesome peers, or beginning to read a self-help book. The **action stage** is when the person is actively doing things to counter the problem: the alcoholic is going to Alcoholics Anonymous, staying out of bars, calling their sponsor, and keeping active. Lastly, in the **maintenance stage**, the person has made the changes and is engaging in actions to ensure the change lasts. There is also, at times, a **relapse stage**, where the person engages in the previous behavior and then cycles back through the stages (but usually quicker the second, third, or fourth time through). See Figure 4.2 for a visual representation of the stages of readiness for change.

You have gone through this process many times previously, without even having realized it. Maybe this was when you experienced some level of depression (not that it had to be diagnosable). At one

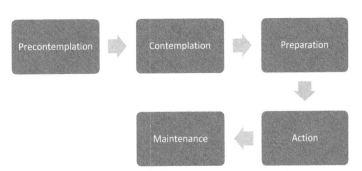

Figure 4.2 People go through various stages on the process of change.

point, you didn't realize you were sad. Then you thought maybe you were, but you waited to see what would happen. When you continued to be sad, you might have searched online for a therapist or looked for a self-help book about overcoming depression. You then started to try to hang out more with friends or maybe even went to see a therapist. Lastly, you found that you weren't depressed anymore and continued doing the things that were working for you, such as going to the gym, hanging out with friends, and journaling. You may currently have days when you feel sad, but you move past it by re-accessing your resources.

Family therapists must understand this process for each person in the therapy room as well as the family as a unit. This may make it more difficult when not everyone in the family is on the same page. One of the key skills to connect everyone in the family is **mutualization**, where the therapist brings together multiple viewpoints into one shared understanding (see Figure 4.3). When people are working toward the same outcome, rather than against one another, they are likely to work harder and more collaboratively.

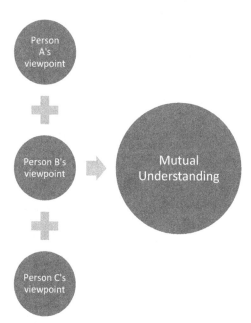

Figure 4.3 Mutualization happens when therapists bridge multiple people's perspectives into one shared understanding.

This skill is quite tricky and takes much craft to pull off as people become wedded to their viewpoints. So, how can you mutualize effectively? For our family coming in because of complaints of an out-of-control teen, the parents want the teen to behave well, while the teen wants the parents off their back. Where is the overlap here? They all want a more peaceful family. The therapist then needs to explore the various aspects of peace for this family and hope that all members buy in. If the goal of therapy remains to change the adolescent, the adolescent may be at the precontemplation or contemplation stage of viewing themselves as being out of control. They will thus likely not engage in activities for change. However, they, as well as the parents, may be at the preparation or action stage when it comes to wanting a peaceful family. If so, there is a greater likelihood that all of them will make active change attempts for this to happen.

Fun Facts

This chapter is about the core competencies and basic therapy skills that family therapists believe are important and necessary for sound practice. But how do family therapists measure whether they are doing well on these competencies? There is a slew of assessments that can be used to determine how well therapists are doing on each of the skills and competencies. These assessments can be self-reports (i.e., the therapist provides responses) or observer reports (e.g., the therapist's supervisor provides responses). Some of these assessments include:

- the Family Therapist Rating Scale;
- the Basic Skills Evaluation Device;
- the Marriage and Family Therapy Internship Evaluation Instrument;
- the Scoring Rubric Counselor-Trainee Clinical Work; and
- the Competency Evaluation Inventory.

There is no single measure (assessment tool) that covers every skill and competency. Further, how well a therapist is doing can also be assessed by the client. Scott Miller developed the Outcome and Session Rating Scales, which clients can fill out to provide the therapist with feedback to better inform treatment. For a more in-depth explanation of the variety of psychometric assessment measures of therapists' skills, please read Perosa and Perosa (2010).

BASIC THERAPY SKILLS

In this section, I briefly present some of the basic therapy skills that family therapists utilize. These are the foundational skills for all therapists and counselors, regardless of which theoretical model or client one is working with (e.g., individual, couple, family, or group). I know this section, and this book, are not sufficient to make you proficient in using these skills. However, this introduction should give you a good sense of how family therapist skills are different from a friend's skills when talking with you.

Empathy

The most common and desired skill of a therapist is to be empathetic. **Empathy** is the ability to understand the thoughts and feelings of another person. As I tell my students in their first class that focuses on these skills, your job is to figure out how it makes sense for *that person* to think, feel, and behave as they do. This doesn't mean you must agree with them. But when you understand where they are coming from, they can understand themselves more deeply and you can then tailor and word your interventions so that they make sense for the client. While you will never be able to do so, empathy is your attempt to walk in your client's shoes.

Empathy has two complementary aspects, one being internal and the other external. Internally, empathy happens when you make sense of the client's experience. You identify their feelings and their viewpoints. Externally, empathy happens when you communicate this understanding to the client. That happens when you engage in active listening, verbally communicating to the client your understanding of their understanding. When you do so accurately, you help strengthen the therapeutic alliance.

People tend not to be in a relationship with someone who is listening empathetically. Rather, when most people go to a friend to talk about a problem, the friend is likely to listen to give advice. Further, the friend doesn't want them to feel bad and will try hard, quite quickly, to make them feel better. But you, as a therapist, must be different. You need to give them the right to feel bad without any attempt to change them (at least right away). I have a crappy visualization to help clarify this distinction between a friend and a therapist. Imagine a large outdoor above-ground pool. In the middle is the person who is in psychological pain. The pool is filled to the brim, not with water, but with fecal matter. It is a crappy situation for everyone involved! What does the therapist do differently than the friend? Hopefully a lot! The friend will stand by the side of the pool with a hose and a towel and tell the person to come over and get out so they can hose them down and then dry them off. This is nice but is usually not that helpful because the *why* of being in the pool is not addressed and the person will likely find themselves back in there in the next few days. The therapist, on the other hand, takes off their shoes and socks, rolls up their pant legs, steps into the pool, walks over to the client, and says, "I'm comfortable sitting in the crap with you." This is when the therapist is really in it with the client.

Active listening occurs by observing and listening to the client's verbal and nonverbal messages and then conveying these back to the client. There are many skills involved in active listening to help move the conversation forward and help the client to understand themselves better. These include the following:

- *Door opener*: This is a statement that gets the client to start to talk about an issue.
  - "Tell me what is most pressing for you today."
- *Minimal encourager*: This is a small verbal or nonverbal communication that tells the client to keep talking.
  - "Okay. Tell me more."
- *Paraphrasing*: This is a reiteration of what the client has told the therapist.
  - "The three of you went to dinner, but once there an argument happened and seemed to get out of control. It got so bad that you left before dessert."
- *Reflections of feeling*: This is an acknowledgment of the emotional content of what the client has said.
  - "You are feeling betrayed because you had agreed on not flirting with anyone else and you found out your partner was texting with someone flirtatiously."
- *Reflections of meaning*: This is an acknowledgment of the value system of the client.
  - "Wow. That was really disappointing for you because you view yourselves as a loving family. And rather than being loving, you found yourselves attacking one another."
- *Questions*: Questions help to bring information into the conversation. There are many different types of questions, including closed, open, swing, and relational. Family therapists utilize

relational (or interactional) questions more than other therapists. These questions ask clients about interpersonal process rather than internal thought processes.

- "When you found out about the infidelity, how did the two of you interact with one another?"
- "What is the typical way that the two of you argue with one another?"
- "How does it typically go with the family when you are trying to decide what to do?"

There is no set order or number of times each of these skills can be used. Like any skill, overuse can become detracting. But these are some of the skills in family therapists' tool pouches that form the basis of their interactions with clients. In the next few chapters, we will cover various models of family therapy. All the practitioners from these models use these basic skills of active listening as they are independent of theory.

From a Student's Perspective

Initially, I thought that family therapy skills were considered more common sense than actual skills, as they are straightforward and not flashy. The straightforwardness made me overly confident that I had already mastered or could quickly master these skills. However, the first time in the therapy room, I learned that it was not as easy as I thought. But once I got the flow of things, those basic skills became reliable. When I feel stuck or unsure of what to do next in a session, I can always rely on these skills to gather more information and strengthen the collaborative conversation that is developing in the room. It took some time for me to grasp and use them effectively, but now these standard skills are the primary tools that I utilize in the therapy room.

Kaitlin Osborne, master's student

DISTINGUISHING BETWEEN CONTENT AND PROCESS

Family therapists like to distinguish themselves from other therapists by focusing primarily on process rather than content. What this means is that they focus on interaction. **Content** is what is said by the family: that Janie cursed at her parents; that Stephen's mother told other family members about Sheila's infidelity; or that the family went to the beach. We cannot avoid content and shouldn't, as it helps contextualize the family's story.

Process refers to how the family interacts. Rather than focusing on Janie's cursing, the family therapist would understand this in terms of the rules of interaction that either allow Janie to curse or are in place to set a hierarchy for her not to do so. Stephen's mother telling other people about the couple's infidelity is information about how open or closed the system is at that point in time. The family going to the beach signals they were able to negotiate with one another to make that happen.

Family members usually pay attention to the content: "… he said …"; "… she told me …"; "… why would he do this …?" Family therapists focus on a higher level of functioning. The family's process is the pathway to their rules, patterns, and homeostasis. If we just tried to problem solve for them about a current argument, they would be back in our office three weeks later with a different argument. What would be the same is *how* they have had the argument. What people argue about is not really that important; the way they argue is. This is because people will always have disagreements. This is inevitable because each person is unique and has their own viewpoints. Focusing on the content would mean the therapist is trying to change a person's viewpoint. Rather, family therapists attempt to change how people communicate with each other when they have differing viewpoints. If you think back to the types of patterned interactions that we discussed in Chapter 3, you can see how this would work with symmetrical relationships. Two people who are used to trying to one-up each other will continue to do so regardless of what the issue is: deciding on a restaurant; whose fault it is they haven't had sex in three months; or how to parent.

When we change the process—the rules of interaction—we change the pattern. This is because a pattern is process over time. Family therapists train themselves to observe the family's process: who turns to whom; who forms alliances or coalitions; who triangulates with whom; etc. Just because it happens once in session doesn't mean this is how it always is at home; but it is likely to be so.

Emotionality

The therapy room is a petri dish of emotionality. People come to therapy knowing it is a context in which they can become highly emotional. So many tears have been shed in a therapist's office that one of the mainstays of the therapy room is a box of tissues.

When working with individuals, there is a skill in what to do when the client gets emotional. Likely, at some point during therapy, the client will cry. What do you do? We call this the **tissue dilemma**. Do you give the client a tissue? For me, this goes back to our swimming pool where you try to sit in the shit with the client. When most people see another person cry, they will give them a tissue, pat them on the back, and tell them it is going to be okay. One of the primary messages that gets sent is, "I am not comfortable with you being uncomfortable so I am going to try to make you comfortable so that I can be comfortable." Usually, the client will reach for the tissue themselves or ask you for one. If they do, give them the box.

When working with families, the issue of emotionality heightens. You have to consider not only each person's emotional reactions, but also what is happening between people (remember, we just talked about this and called it the family's process). Families tend to come to therapy when things are not going well. They are sometimes extremely upset and mad at one another. One of their ways of handling these feelings is through yelling, cursing, or even getting physically violent. I've had sessions where brothers fist-fought with one another, mother and adult daughter screamed at one another, and husband and wife cursed at one another. This is going to happen when you work with families. The question is: what are you going to do when this happens? This is another skill of therapy that family therapists must have in their tool pouch that individual therapists do not. Some therapists will want to decrease emotionality while others will want to increase it.

Those family therapists that want to decrease emotionality can do this in a variety of ways. The main way is to have family members talk to you rather than each other. When they are highly charged because they have been ticked off by another family member, if they speak directly to that person, there is a greater risk of escalation. You have likely experienced this when you were so upset with someone, you told them: "Look, I need to take a breather; otherwise I'm likely to say something that I'll regret." Having family members talk to you rather than each other gives people room to breathe, as the non-talking family members can sit and observe what is happening. This process is designed to reduce the anxiety in the room so that people can more readily access their cognitive processes. We will talk about the importance of this in the next chapter. Another tool to decrease emotionality is the talking stick (or some other such talisman), where the rule is that only the person holding the object can talk.

However, family therapists more often than not try to increase emotionality. This is because they want the family's typical process to come out in the session so that it is more readily identifiable and thus changeable. For those trying to increase emotionality, the aim is to encourage people to safely express themselves when they are normally holding back. You should never try to increase emotionality so that people physically hurt one another; but there are times when you want to see what their arguments look like, and you will encourage them to have the argument in front of you. We call this technique **enactment**. When you engage the family in enactment, they are having their argument under your direction. You can then stop them at various points and highlight what the process is:

- "Hold on a second. Something very interesting just happened. When mother and daughter disagreed, dad entered the conversation to back up mom. How come that happened?"
- "Did you all notice that dad and son were arguing, and son tried to get mom to support his position? How often does that happen?"

This type of processing of the family's process brings it out into the foreground and gives it a new context.

As you can see, family therapists need to have a wide array of skills and tools available to them so they can adhere to and achieve the vast number of competencies the field expects of them. This isn't a profession where therapists can say and do whatever they want without any focus. We are dealing with people's emotions, experiences, and lives. This is a very serious endeavor. We need to do so ethically (see Chapter 2), as well as competently. Hopefully this chapter has provided you an initial understanding of the core competencies and skills that family therapists need to have at their disposal.

GLOSSARY

- **Active listening**: The process of understanding a client's statements and letting them know this understanding.
- **Burnout**: Emotional exhaustion from doing something over and over.

- **Compassion fatigue**: Wanting so much to help someone else and being overwhelmed by this effort.
- **Competency**: The ability to do something well.
- **Content**: The "facts" of what was said or occurred.
- **Countertransference**: When the therapist's personal issues become present in the therapeutic process.
- **Empathy**: The ability to experience another person's thoughts and feelings psychologically and/or emotionally.
- **Enactment**: When the therapist gets at least two family members to interact with one another during the session.
- **Joining**: The process of the therapist connecting with the client to form a therapeutic relationship.
- **Mutualization**: Exploring how various family members' positions overlap.
- **Neutrality**: The therapeutic position of not taking any one family member's side.
- **Process**: The way in which people interact with one another.
- **Reflexivity**: The process of assessing oneself and being thoughtful about what one does.
- **Self-care**: Engaging in activities to ensure one is physically, psychologically, and emotionally well.
- **Self-of-the-therapist**: The understanding that a therapist is a person who has thoughts, beliefs, feelings, and experiences which impact how they engage in the therapeutic process.
- **Therapeutic relationship**: The connection between therapist and client.
- **Wounded healers**: People who became therapists because they wanted to get over past hurts.

CHAPTER SUMMARY

- Family therapists are expected to be competent, having knowledge and skills in a variety of areas.
- The self-of-the-therapist is an important competency, as the person of the therapist impacts how they understand and influence the therapeutic process.
- Joining is the process of making a connection with the client, which is extremely important, as it is the medium through which client change happens.

- Family therapists understand that not all clients come to therapy with the same motivation to change and work with each client differently based on their readiness for change.
- The basic therapy skills of empathic understanding, distinguishing between content and process, and handling emotionality are some of the most useful family therapy skills.
- Family therapists use basic skills such as door openers, minimal encouragers, paraphrasing, reflections of feeling, reflections of meaning, and questions to help expand the conversation.

REFERENCES

Duncan, B. L., Miller, S. D., & Sparks, J. A. (2004). *The heroic client.* Jossey-Bass.

Miller, S. D., Hubble, M. A., & Chow, D. (2020). *Better results: Using deliberate practice to improve therapeutic effectiveness.* American Psychological Association.

Prochaska, J. O., Norcross, J. C., and DiClimente, C. C. (2013). Applying the stages of change. In G. P. Koocher, J. C. Norcross, & B. A. Greene (Eds.). *Psychologists' desk reference* (3rd ed.) (pp. 176–181). Oxford University Press.

INTERGENERATIONAL FAMILY THERAPIES

ORIENTING QUESTIONS

* What is the focus of intergenerational family therapies?
* How does a Bowenian (natural systems perspective) understand how people negotiate the anxiety of individuality and togetherness?
* How does an appreciation of relational ethics assist contextual family therapists in helping families to change?

We now start to get into the particular models of family therapy that help us to conceptualize families, in terms of why they are having their current problems and what we can do in the therapy room to help them get better. In this chapter, we discuss **intergenerational models**, which focus on how multiple generations of families of origin impact each other over time. While there are several intergenerational models, we focus on the two most prominent ones: Bowen's natural systems theory and Boszormenyi-Nagy's contextual therapy.

BOWEN'S NATURAL SYSTEMS THEORY

Murray Bowen was a psychiatrist who began studying schizophrenic individuals. He eventually had their families come to live on the hospital grounds where he worked, to observe their unique patterns of interaction. Basing his ideas on evolutionary theory, Bowen eventually developed perhaps the most in-depth conceptualization of how families function and how individuals have symptoms. This approach

DOI: 10.4324/9781003312536-5

is sometimes called Bowen theory, Bowen therapy, or natural systems theory.

Major Players

Murray Bowen (1913–1990) received his M.D. from the University of Tennessee in 1934. He was a psychiatrist who initially worked at the Menninger Foundation and then the National Institute of Mental Health. He would have families with a schizophrenic child come to live on the hospital grounds so he could observe them. Using evolutionary concepts, Bowen developed his model, natural systems theory (now called Bowen theory), which he thought applied to all living systems, not just humans. Bowen was the originator and first president of the American Family Therapy Association. Toward the latter part of his career, Bowen worked at the Georgetown University Medical Center and founded the Family Center. Today, the **Bowen Center for the Study of the Family** is a major trainer and contributor in Bowen theory. Bowen's most influential book is *Family Evaluation*, co-written with Michael Kerr.

Why Families Have Problems

Bowen hypothesized that all living systems function based on two equally important competing life forces: **individuality** and **togetherness** (see Figure 5.1). While he viewed natural systems theory as relevant for any living system (e.g., bees, elephants, forests), we will talk about the model only in reference to human beings. People have a need to be separate while being connected. Too much pull in either direction is problematic.

People experience anxiety when trying to navigate the landscape of individuality and togetherness. This is a different anxiety than you think about when you give a public speech or take an exam. In Bowen theory, therapists focus on **chronic anxiety**, an automatic

Figure 5.1 People have two competing life forces: individuality and togetherness.

biological function that happens when the individual is in situations that push or pull them toward individuality or togetherness. Bowen distinguished between the relational system and the emotional system. The relational system is what happens between people (i.e., that mother tried to connect to daughter; that father does not speak to his father). What Bowenians focus more on is the **emotional system**: the *why* of those interconnections. It is this emotional system that is the principal force in why people have problems.

The family is an emotional unit and family members are connected to one another over time. By "emotional," Bowenians are not referring to feelings such as being happy, sad, mad, or glad. Rather, this is an emotional interdependence whereby people are connected to one another in a reciprocal interaction. Without thinking about it, people are reactively connected, experiencing the chronic anxiety of being separate yet together. To help explain this process, Bowen developed eight interlocking concepts: differentiation of self; triangles; nuclear family emotional process; family projection process; multigenerational transmission process; emotional cutoff; sibling position; and societal emotional process. Each of these concepts is explored below.

Differentiation of Self

Differentiation of self is the best-known concept in Bowen theory and refers to a person's ability to be thoughtful rather than reactive. When a person has a less developed self, they are more likely to be impacted by other people and/or will more likely try to control the functioning of others. This person has difficulty taking an **I position**. Rather, they rely on other people to help them form opinions or make choices. They also struggle when others do not agree with them and attempt to push others to think similarly.

A person with a well-developed self can define for themselves what they want while also allowing others to define themselves. This does not mean that the individual does not consider other people. They may do things that other people want when they themselves do not. However, they do so because they have carefully thought about the situation. In essence, they are using their thinking system rather than emotional reactivity to guide them. A well-differentiated person is not a selfish person. They think about what their own thoughts, feelings, and needs are, as well as those of the other person. They then make choices based on what they think is best in that situation.

Bowen believed that a person's level of differentiation is grounded on building blocks from birth, but the emotional system they are born into helps develop their self. Once developed, a person's level of differentiation stays fairly constant throughout their life. It takes active thoughtful effort to change one's differentiation, which is what Bowen therapy is focused on.

Triangles

As seen in this theory, people don't like to experience anxiety and try to bind it (to relieve it). They may do this with the person they are trying to gain either some separation from or some connectedness to. When this does not resolve the anxiety, they tend to bring in a third person to offset this anxiety. This process is called **triangulation** (see Figure 5.2). Bowen believed that in times of calm, a two-person system is functional. However, when anxiety increases, it quickly becomes unstable. Thus, he held that the three-person system is the smallest stable unit.

You have triangulated other people and/or been triangulated thousands of times throughout your life; you just never realized it was happening or what it was called. How many times have you had an argument with a significant other, family member, or friend where you ended the interaction still upset with each another? What is the first thing you did when that person wasn't around? I can guess that you likely called or went to another person to complain about the first person. Your conversation probably started with: "You'll never believe what [the person you had the argument with] did/said ..." You also probably chose to contact someone you thought would take your side. This then helped relieve your anxiety, at least temporarily.

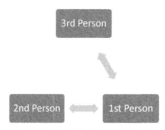

Figure 5.2 When two people have difficulty resolving anxiety between them, at least one member tends to triangulate a third party.

Triangles are good for anxiety reduction in the short term. However, in the long term, they tend to be problematic because the processes that were initially in play are still there. Neither member grew (became better differentiated, if only in the minutest way). Triangulation tends to be a problematic process; however, as we will see, in Bowen therapy sessions, being involved in triangles doesn't always have to be bad.

Nuclear Family Emotional Process

In the nuclear family—whether a single-parent, blended, or other formation—there are four primary ways that people engage each other to try to bind anxiety. These basic relationship patterns, which all families exhibit in one way or another, are known as the **nuclear family emotional process**. These are marital conflict; dysfunction in a spouse; impairment of one or more children; and emotional distance.

During times of stress, relationship partners may begin to focus their energies on each other, particularly looking at what the other person is doing wrong. This way of dealing with anxiety produces **marital conflict**. Each person tries to control, while trying not to be controlled by, the other. A related process is when only one of the partners externalizes their anxiety on the other. This pattern, known as **dysfunction in a spouse**, occurs when one partner continuously gives in to the other. This can be okay when chronic and situational anxiety are not that high; however, when the anxiety increases too much, one spouse may develop physical or psychological symptoms.

Rather than focusing their energies on a spouse, the adults may try to bind their anxiety on their children. This usually happens by worrying too much about a child, where the child then develops an impairment. This **impairment in one or more children** can be seen in interpersonal, intrapersonal, and behavioral symptoms. Lastly, family members may try to deal with anxiety through **emotional distance**. When anxiety increases, people may psychologically and physically distance themselves to reduce the intensity. There is a risk here that people will distance too much.

These four basic relationship patterns are problematic in that they continue people's ways of being with each another that maintain or perpetuate the likelihood that one or more people in the emotional system will become symptomatic. Because people try to bind their anxiety, and sometimes successfully do so, it usually comes at the expense of someone else. For instance, when parents lessen their anxiety by focusing their energies on a child, the child must absorb anxiety.

Family Projection Process

As we've been discussing, the emotional system is the medium in which anxiety is transmitted in a family. If we look at what happens intergenerationally between parents and children, we can then focus on the **family projection process**. This process follows three steps. First, the parent(s) focus on one (or more) of their children, fearing that something is wrong with that child. Second, the child behaves in a way that confirms the fear of the parent. Third, the parent then reacts to the child as if something is truly wrong with them. In essence, a self-fulfilling prophecy arises, where the parent believes there is something wrong with the child and this fear (and the reaction of people around it) leads to the development of symptoms.

While the family projection process may happen to multiple children in a family, there is likely one—for whatever reason—where it is more intense. This may be based on birth order, gender, adoption status, or other factors such as a child born with a disability.

From a Student's Perspective

Like any new voyage to a new world and meeting new people, Bowen family system theory was foreign to me but somehow fascinating, because it allowed me to observe the human family as a living system. Though the journey was not easy, being able to see how individual behavior influences each other in complex ways was interesting and led to my curiosity to observe how each member of a family unit's happiness, health, ability to communicate and contribution to society are intertwined and impacted by their interdependence. A differentiated self was the key component that helped me, as a person and therapist, to be able to function emotionally separated while sustaining meaningful relationships with others. Bowen family system therapy has helped me bring awareness to others who have now learned that they are creating another episode in an ongoing series. This has helped them significantly in reorganizing the emotional system within their families.

Georgieann Neal, doctoral student

Multigenerational Transmission Process

Bowen theory views what happens in families across multiple generations. The idea is that people in a family develop more or less the same level of differentiation as one another. People tend to partner with someone at a similar differentiation level. Their children, based on being born and raised within that emotional system, develop similar differentiation levels. However, as seen in the family projection process, one child is likely to be the focus of the parents' anxiety and will be less differentiated. Another child may perhaps be slightly more differentiated.

When these children grow up, they will each partner with someone at the same differentiation level. Their children will experience the family projection process, with one developing slightly higher levels of differentiation and one lower (it may be multiple higher and/or lower depending on the number of children, but for example's sake I am using just two children). This happens generation after generation and, taken altogether, is called the **multigenerational transmission process** (see Figure 5.3).

As you can see, one branch of the family will slowly increase the level of differentiation of most of its members while another branch will slowly decrease the level of differentiation. Therefore, Bowen thought that in every family, within seven generations, severe symptoms will be seen in one or more members. This is likely the branch of the family on whom the family projection process has had the most significant impact and who have experienced high chronic anxiety and low levels of differentiation.

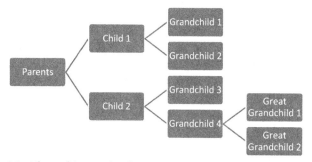

Figure 5.3   The multigenerational transmission process describes how, over successive generations, parents transmit slightly higher or lower levels of differentiation to their children.

Emotional Cutoff

As explained, people try to reduce tension and anxiety. Sometimes they can do this well, which enhances both individuals. However, when people feel the push or pull of individuality and togetherness and cannot easily resolve it, they may engage in **emotional cutoff**, where they reduce their contact with the other person. This can be taken to an extreme where a person moves away from home and never contacts their family again. However, you can live in the same house as someone and engage in emotional cutoff. This would be by not psychologically engaging with them, where interactions remain superficial.

Emotional cutoff is a good short-term way of decreasing anxiety. However, the patterns that led to the anxiety are likely still there. Imagine that you can't stand the tension between yourself and your parent. You decide to move across the country and limit contact with them because there are too many arguments. You then begin dating someone and all is well—until, that is, an argument happens. You have not learned how to stay engaged when there is tension. You are likely to end this relationship much more quickly than if you had learned how to try to negotiate with someone and stay in contact even when there is disagreement.

Sibling Position

Based on the research of Walter Toman, Bowen incorporated the notion of sibling position into his theory. Depending on where one falls in the sibling order, there are different typical characteristics. For instance, older children tend to be more responsible and hold leadership positions, while younger siblings are a little more playful and tend to be followers. While there is a chronological position (e.g., firstborn, middle child, youngest), what is more important is the functional sibling position—that is, the role someone takes regardless of age. For instance, if the firstborn has some type of physical or intellectual deficit, the middle child may functionally act like the oldest child and be the most responsible in the sibling group.

Societal Emotional Process

The last of Bowen's eight interlocking concepts describes how the emotional system functions within societies. The **societal emotional**

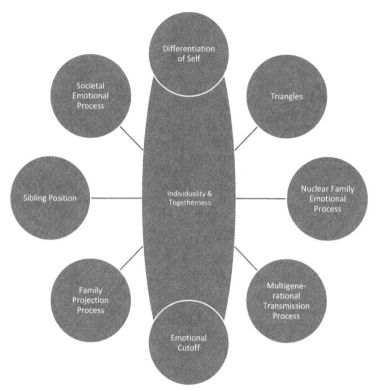

Figure 5.4 Bowen proposed eight interlocking concepts that regulate the degree of individuality and togetherness family members experience within the emotional system.

process holds that due to shifting cultural forces, human societies go through periods of progression and regression. In essence, our lenses of exploring issues of individuality and togetherness are widened, so we look beyond what happens in a nuclear family or a family of origin and see how these processes unfold in larger social groups. Figure 5.4 presents a visual of these eight interlocking concepts.

Fun Facts

The Bowen Center for the Study of the Family is the leading center for the furthering of the ideas Murray Bowen developed. Starting in 1965, Bowen's graduating residents hosted the Annual Symposium for Family Theory and Family Psychotherapy. This symposium continues today, with leading individuals from around the world coming together to further develop Bowenian ideas. In 1969, Bowen began a Postgraduate Program in Bowen Family Systems Theory and its Applications; and then in 1975, he founded the Georgetown University Family Center. In 1990, the Center separated from Georgetown University to operate on its own. That same year, Dr. Bowen died and Dr. Michael Kerr took over the directorship. Kerr co-wrote with Bowen the most influential book on Bowen theory, *Family Evaluation*. The center eventually changed its name to The Bowen Center for the Study of the Family, where they engage in training and education around Bowen theory.

How Problems Get Solved

Bowen held that all people are potentially symptomatic. Further, a person with a higher level of differentiation may become symptomatic before a person with a lower level of differentiation. This is because we also must understand how much anxiety is in the system. The more anxiety in the system, the higher the levels of differentiation needed to be able to bind one's anxiety.

Given this, there are two basic goals in Bowen therapy (see Figure 5.5). First, the therapist tries to decrease anxiety so that people are better able to utilize their cognitive system rather than their reactive system. In essence, the therapist attempts to get people to use their heads rather than their guts. The more people can calmly and intellectually examine a situation, the more they can freely choose to behave rather than unconsciously react.

Second, Bowen therapists try to help each member they contact to increase their level of differentiation—that is, to help people make their own determinations and choices while still being connected to others. The primary position the Bowen therapist takes is that of a **coach**, where they help the client to explore their family of origin, see the primary relationship patterns, and then go back to

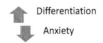

Differentiation

Anxiety

Figure 5.5   Bowen therapists attempt to increase people's level of differentiation while also decreasing their level of anxiety.

their family of origin to detriangulate from the various interlocking triangles that all families have.

Genograms

The most famous tool of Bowen therapy is the **genogram**: a family diagram that depicts the facts and functioning of a family across several generations. Usually, a genogram contains at least three generations. In therapy, the therapist interviews the family and visually depicts who is in the family and the primary relationship patterns happening for them. This provides a visual understanding of the emotional system.

In a session, the therapist develops the genogram with the client and then explores the various patterns. The process of doing so helps the client shift from relying on their reactivity to using their cognitive system. In a typical genogram, males are depicted with squares and females with circles. Three generations are desired, as this helps demonstrate some of the common interpersonal intergenerational patterns.

Figure 5.6 presents a genogram of a family with a mother and father and two children. The adult daughter is divorced, had a

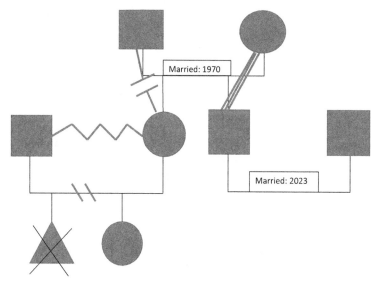

Figure 5.6 A sample genogram, depicting the members of a family along with their relationship qualities.

miscarriage, and has a daughter. The adult son recently married his partner. Father and daughter are cut off from one another. Adult daughter has a conflictual relationship with her ex-husband. Mother and son have a very close relationship. Genograms will usually be in much greater detail, but this one is provided here to give you an initial sense of what a genogram may look like.

Detriangulating

The Bowen therapist enters the family as a nonreactive third party—a process called **detriangulating**. People usually try to triangulate others to help reduce their own anxiety. The Bowen therapist attempts to stay neutral and not take sides in a family. Rather, they get the family members to validate themselves, where each person assesses their own thoughts and actions. The more the therapist can stay engaged and neutral, even when anxiety increases, the more people can find new ways of being with one another.

To be able to stay connected to families during times of stress and anxiety, the therapist must maintain a position of neutrality. To do so, they must have actively worked on their own level of differentiation. Thus, on their own, Bowen therapists spend a lot of time exploring their own family dynamics. Similar to psychoanalysts going through their own analysis, Bowen therapists tend to do their own family-of-origin work so they are less reactive and more thoughtful during sessions. This allows them to maintain their cognitive functioning during therapy sessions, which can be filled with high levels of anxiety.

CONTEXTUAL THERAPY

Contextual therapy is an intergenerational approach developed by Ivan Boszormenyi-Nagy that focuses on the relational ethics that accrue between people. This ethic attempts to get all members of a family to act in the best interests of everyone, not just themselves.

Major Players

Ivan Boszormenyi-Nagy (1920–2007) was born in Budapest, Hungary into a family of prominent judges. He earned his degree in psychiatry from Peter Pazmany University. He subsequently left

Hungary because of his dislike of working for Communist loyalists and eventually moved to the United States in 1950. In 1957, he began working at the Eastern Pennsylvania Psychiatric Institute, where he researched more effective ways of working with schizophrenics and their families. He eventually developed **contextual therapy**. Perhaps his biggest contribution to the field was the introduction of the concept of relational ethics, which focuses on the notion of fairness. For almost 20 years, he served as chief of the Family Therapy Section in the Department of Psychiatry at Hahnemann University (now known as Drexel University); and he was a founding member of the American Family Therapy Academy. Boszormenyi-Nagy also founded the Institute for Contextual Growth—a training institute that helped disseminate the ideas of contextual therapy. His most influential books include *Between Give and Take* and *Invisible Loyalties*.

Why Families Have Problems

Nagy initially proposed four basic dimensions of relational reality: factual predeterminants; human psychology; communications and transactions; and relational ethics. More recently, a fifth dimension has been included in the theory: the ontic dimension (see Figure 5.6). In this section, we explore each of these dimensions.

Dimension I: Facts focuses on those aspects of human existence that just are, such as historical facts, physical health, and the events of a person's life. That someone is a middle child, they have blond hair, their parents divorced, and they were born and raised in Thailand are all facts.

Dimension II: Psychology explores the internal functioning of an individual. This is where we can look at their emotional and psychological wellbeing, hopes and goals, as well as their feelings, beliefs, and motivations. For any of you who are/were psychology majors, you can use much of what you learned in "Introduction to Psychology" (and upper-level courses) to understand someone's functioning.

Dimension III: Family Systems describes the interpersonal transactions occurring in the family. This incorporates many of the concepts of systems theory that were discussed in Chapter 3. These include alliances, coalitions, boundaries, rules, patterns, homeostasis, etc.

Dimension IV: Relational Ethics is the core of contextual therapy, highlighting how people balance the give and take in human interactions. There is an ethic of **due consideration**, where there should be equity in interactions. In essence, this is the Golden Rule: do unto others as you would have them do unto you. When a person shows concern for someone else, they earn **merit**, also known as **entitlement**. When you give to someone (it doesn't have to be a gift or money, but perhaps a call to check in or a ride to the airport if they need it), you receive as well. People will give without expecting something in return from the other person, but usually only up to a point. A relationship can't be totally one-sided. When both people give due consideration to the other, they each earn **constructive entitlement**, which enriches both of their lives. And what they give need not be the same. For instance, one person can give by being there to listen to the other person; while the other person gives through acts of service, such as errands or cooking.

However, problems arise when a person's **ledger** becomes unbalanced. People have an unconscious ledger that weighs how much they have given to and received from a person. When the ledger is unbalanced for a length of time with someone, difficulties may arise (see Figure 5.7).

Destructive entitlement happens when a person expects to be given to from someone who has not accrued the debt. You know this situation when you begin to date someone and realize that they "have baggage." What that means is they are not over what happened in a previous relationship. Perhaps they loved the person and gave everything to the relationship, but didn't get much back. They stayed in it because they thought they could change the person, but it didn't work out that way. Eventually, they couldn't take any more and ended the relationship. They then come into their new relationship with you unconsciously (or consciously) thinking, "I gave so much previously and didn't get much back. In this relationship, I am not going to give until I receive first." They expect you to give more than you should, to make up for what someone else didn't give them. If you do so, eventually you will find that your own ledger is unbalanced. You may then end the relationship and expect your next partner to give more than they owe you. If left unchecked, this process of destructive entitlement can spread through the web of interconnections.

Destructive entitlement can also happen in relation to groups. Take a person whose facts are that they were born into a family that was quite poor, where both parents were drug addicts who divorced soon

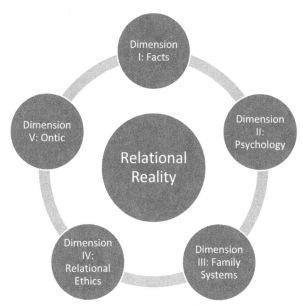

Figure 5.7 A person's relational reality is based on five basic dimensions.

after their birth; and they were born with a disability. This person may believe the world owes them, since they were not given the benefits that many other people have. They may then act toward people in ways that include expectations beyond what is normally expected of others.

Another aspect of relational ethics involves **loyalty**, which is when we put the interests of people who have shown us due concern over those who haven't. Contextual therapists look at this on the vertical and horizontal planes. **Vertical loyalty** focuses on one's family of origin, with those above us being our parents and grandparents and those below us being our children. **Horizontal loyalty** focuses on one's partner or peers (see Figure 5.8).

At times, we may experience loyalty conflicts, since we are indebted to multiple people. A partner may become angry that we are showing more due concern for a work colleague than we are for them. A parent may expect an adult child to side with them rather than the spouse. Perhaps the most destructive loyalty conflict is when a child feels they must choose between parents, which puts them into a **split loyalty**.

Figure 5.8 People keep an internal ledger of what they have given and received from individuals. People prefer to have balanced ledgers.

Usually, these loyalty issues arise outside of people's awareness. These invisible loyalties lead to destructive entitlements, where people try to gain someone's love in a way that leads to intrapersonal and/or interpersonal symptoms.

Dimension V: Ontic was the last dimension to be developed and the least that is fully explored. It discusses how a person's self is developed in relation to others. It establishes who you are by who you are not. For instance, say your father was extremely overbearing with you. As an adult, you may tell yourself, "I am not going to parent like my father did. I am going to give my child freedom."

How Problems Get Solved

Contextual therapy is designed to help people balance their ledgers and shift from destructive to constructive entitlement. The primary position the therapist takes is that of **multidirected partiality**, where they consider the perspective of every member of the family that is in the room, as well as all of those not in the room who are in the relational web of the family. This is because if a person's ledger is unbalanced, they will likely negatively impact another person, who will negatively impact another etc.

In therapy, the contextual therapist helps family members balance their ledgers to achieve **acknowledgment**, where people come to

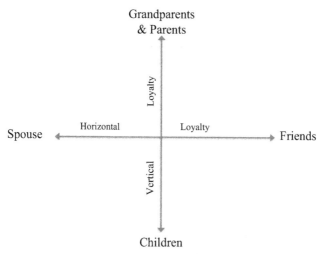

Figure 5.9 Loyalty is both vertical and horizontal. We are indebted to multiple people, which may lead to loyalty conflicts.

understand how they and others have tried to show due concern to one another. One aspect of this is **exoneration**, which happens when a person attempts to acknowledge and be fair with someone whom they believe has wronged them. This can be very difficult for some people, as they might see the other person as a monster. The other has likely treated them in very negative ways. Exoneration helps unfold the context in which that person acted that led them to behave in problematic ways. It is not about saying that those behaviors were okay or good. Rather, it holds that people are victims of their circumstances. When people acknowledge that another person was behaving based on the context they were in, this can help prevent the current destructive entitlement.

This process of **rejunction** helps people to ethically relate to one another. The more people can give without expecting in return and receive what someone else wants to give, the more they can develop fairness and trust in the relationship. People don't show due concern in the same way. For instance, for my 40th birthday, my wife organized a surprise party for me. I don't know how many hours and how much energy it took to keep this secret (which she and everyone else did), but I thought it was a very nice gesture. It was just one of many ways she has shown me due concern. The interesting part of it for me, in relation to contextual therapy, is that she and I have the same birthday, so the party could have been for her as well. I'm not sure many guests realized this. During the party, she said to me, "Don't you ever dare do this to me!" For me, receiving a surprise party was a sign of her caring. For her, not receiving a surprise party was a sign of my caring. And you better believe she has not, and will not, receive one from me (just chocolates, which I know she will receive as a sign of my caring). I give this example to highlight that people are not always open to the ways other people try to show concern. Rather, they expect to receive back exactly what they give (e.g., "I gave you money so you must give me money"; "I listened when you had problems so you must listen to my problems"). People want to give and to receive in different ways. Contextual therapy helps open the ways of doing so.

One of these ways is to help family members to have **genuine dialogue** with each another. That is, they engage one another based on equity, where they take their own and the other person's rights and needs into consideration. Contextual therapists try not to focus on pathology but rather on people's **relational resources**: those factual and relational connections that people have that can help them develop trustworthy relationships. The end goal is a balancing of ledgers where people are acting in a relationally ethical way in all their relationships.

GLOSSARY

- **Acknowledgment**: Understanding how others have tried to show due concern.
- **Chronic anxiety**: An automatic biological function based on the push and pull of individuality and togetherness.
- **Constructive entitlement**: Occurs when a person takes into consideration how their actions affect other people.
- **Destructive entitlement**: Expecting others to owe you when they have not accrued the debt.
- **Detriangulating**: The process of staying connected with two individuals without taking sides or being reactive.
- **Differentiation of self**: A person's ability to be thoughtful rather than reactive—that is, they can make conscious choice of action.

- **Due consideration**: An ethic that there should be equity in interactions.
- **Emotional cutoff**: When a person cannot handle the current anxiety, they will emotionally, psychologically, or physically distance themselves from others.
- **Emotional system**: The concept that the family is connected via the competing life forces of individuality and togetherness.
- **Entitlement**: Earned merit with a particular person, based on having shown due concern to them.
- **Exoneration**: Attempting to acknowledge the actions of a person who has wronged you.
- **Family projection process**: The process of passing on the parents' differentiation to their children.
- **Genogram**: A pictorial representation of the family that usually covers at least three generations, highlighting the emotional connections and disconnections of family members.
- **Genuine dialogue**: When two people can relate to one another with equity, considering each of their rights and needs.
- **Horizontal loyalty**: Preferential attachment to one's spouse, friends, coworkers, etc. (not blood relatives).
- **Intergenerational models**: Family therapy models that explore the theory of problem formation and problem resolution as occurring over multiple generations.
- **Loyalty**: Preferential attachment to certain relational partners.
- **Merit**: When a person shows concern for someone else.
- **Multidirected partiality**: Attitude and method of considering the impact that one's interventions have on everyone who will encounter the clients.
- **Multigenerational transmission process**: The process of how an emotional system occurs across multiple generations.
- **Nuclear family emotional process**: The basic relational patterns that families exhibit when attempting to deal with anxiety.
- **Rejunction**: The process of helping people relate ethically to one another.
- **Relational ethics**: A contextual principle that explores the balance between give and take for an individual.
- **Relational resources**: The factual and relational connections that people can use to help them relate ethically to others.

- **Split loyalty**: A destructive process in which a child feels forced to choose between their parents.
- **Triangulation**: When anxiety cannot be resolved between two people, one or both involve a third party to try to offset the anxiety.
- **Vertical loyalty**: Preferential attachment to one's parents and/or children.

CHAPTER SUMMARY

- Bowen therapy is based on natural systems theory, which holds that eight interlocking concepts are present in all natural systems.
- Bowenians explore a person's emotional system, in which there is a struggle between being an individual and staying connected to others.
- The most famous concept in Bowen theory is differentiation of self, which is a person's ability to be thoughtful rather than reactive.
- Bowenian therapists attempt to get people to understand the historical relational dynamics in their families so they can be thoughtful in their choice of interactions rather than being reactive.
- Contextual therapy is best known for introducing the concept of relational ethics into the family therapy field—where there should be a balancing of what one has earned and what one owes someone else.
- Contextual therapy rests on five dimensions: facts; psychology; family systems; relational ethics; and ontic.
- Contextual therapists take a position of multidirected partiality, where they consider the position of all parties who are impacted by the actions of those in the therapy room.
- Contextual therapy attempts to help people through the rejunction process, where they are better able to relate ethically to one another.

REFERENCES

Boszormenyi-Nagy, I., & Krasner, B. R. (1986). *Between give and take*. Brunner/Mazel.

Boszormenyi-Nagy, I., & Spark, G. (1984). *Invisible loyalties*. Brunner/Mazel.

Kerr, M. E., & Bowen, M. (1988). *Family evaluation*. Norton.

EXPERIENTIAL FAMILY THERAPIES

ORIENTING QUESTIONS

- What are the benefits of focusing on the here-and-now experiences for clients?
- How does Satir's Growth Model help family members to communicate with one another in a more congruent manner?
- What aspects of symbolic-experiential family therapy help expand family members' ways of being with one another?

Experiential family therapies focus on the here and now, challenging families to move from past complaints to current experiences. By being genuine and present in the moment, people develop greater access to their full selves. This enables them to accept themselves more and to accept others more as well. Rather than being rigid and manualized, experiential therapies highlight the importance of the person of the therapist as they engage in human interactions with their clients. It is this real connection that is the medium for change and growth. Sessions are spontaneous and geared toward the uniqueness of each family. This chapter covers the two most significant experiential family therapies: Virginia Satir's Growth Model and Carl Whitaker's symbolic-experiential family therapy.

Satir's Growth Model

Virginia Satir is one of the most prominent figures in the history of family therapy. Her hands-on approach, along with her deep-set belief in the possibilities of people, made her one of the most beloved founders of family therapy. Her approach, known as the Satir Growth Model (also called the human validation process movement), inspired

DOI: 10.4324/9781003312536-6

thousands of therapists to help individuals and families to reach their full potential.

Major Players

Virginia Satir (1916–1988) was a larger-than-life figure in the history of family therapy. Satir graduated from the Milwaukee State Teachers College (now the University of Wisconsin) in 1936 and was a public school teacher, where she realized the impact of parents on students' performance. In 1948 she earned a master's in social work from the University of Chicago. In the late 1950s, she joined Jackson, Haley, and others in developing the Mental Research Institute (MRI). Satir wrote one of the first books about family therapy, *Conjoint Family Therapy*, in which she provided transcripts of how she worked. Satir left the MRI to move to Esalen and eventually developed the **Avanta Network**, which included practitioners who operated from her model, sometimes called the **human process validation movement** or the **Satir Growth Model**. She focused on the wholeness of the person and helped people move from positions of low self-esteem to become authentic and congruent. Toward the end of her life, Satir utilized her ideas on a more national and international level, working with larger groups to help move toward peace.

Why Families Have Problems

Every person has resources available to them; but when troubled, they do not usually utilize these resources to their utmost abilities. This holistic concept separates the Satir Growth Model from other family therapies. To help provide a visual, Satir described this concept through a **self-mandala**, with the individual at the center. Surrounding them are the eight universal human resources: spiritual, contextual, nutritional, interactional, sensual, emotional, intellectual, and physical (see Figure 6.1).

Many people view these parts as separate from one another. Rather, they should be viewed as interconnected. The more that each aspect of self is focused on, the healthier the person and the better able they are to engage others from a genuine and caring position. When one or more aspects of self are not accounted for, the person is not in balance. This leads to a blockage in the flow of energy within the person. This usually comes out in the form of symptoms, where the person is not aware of themselves and how they are trying to

Figure 6.1 The self-mandala consists of eight components that all influence the wellbeing of the person.

accommodate being imbalanced and incongruent. In essence, the less these eight areas are privileged, the lower the person's self-esteem.

When people experience low self-esteem, they attempt to cope in ways they are likely to be unaware of. Satir called these coping strategies **survival stances**. These stances help people temporarily deal with presumed threats and protect their self-worth. In the short term, these stances do help protect us. However, they do not help us—or other people—to grow and thrive. The four survival stances are placating, blaming, super-reasonable, and irrelevant.

The **placating** survival stance occurs when people discount themselves and privilege the other person and the context (see Figure 6.2). In essence, they give in to what the other person wants, disregarding their own preferences. To get along, they give up self. The individual tends to apologize a lot, feels worthless, and may become depressed or suicidal. On the positive side, they tend to be quite sensitive and caring.

Figure 6.2   The placating stance discounts self and privileges the other person and the context.

Figure 6.3   The blaming stance discounts the other person and privileges self and context.

Figure 6.4   The super-reasonable stance discounts self and other and privileges the context.

The **blaming** survival stance privileges self and context while discounting the other (see Figure 6.3). To cope with low self-esteem, the person attacks another individual. While on the outside the individual seems quite assertive, on the inside they feel very isolated and alone. Their experience leads them to sometimes feel paranoid and even potentially homicidal.

The **super-reasonable** survival stance privileges the context and discounts the self and other (see Figure 6.4). This person focuses on

Figure 6.5 The irrelevant stance discounts self, other, and context.

the rules rather than on emotions and relationships. They are very data driven and people might appreciate them for their intellect. To offset their internal vulnerability, the super-reasonable person doesn't allow themselves to connect with any emotions. This can lead to a rigidness that may be displayed via obsessive-compulsive behaviors.

The **irrelevant** survival stance discounts self, other, and context (see Figure 6.5). They engage in distraction to avoid having to deal with their low self-esteem. People might describe them as fun and spontaneous. However, you cannot have a serious or straightforward conversation with them. This leads to a psychological orientation of confusion and possible psychosis.

The goal of Satir's therapy is to help people enhance their own and others' self-esteem. When we do so, we function from a **congruent** communication stance. This is the healthiest position we can operate from.

Fun Facts

Virginia Satir developed the Avanta Network in 1977 to help teach people how to connect with one another and achieve their full potential. The word "Avanta" means to move forward. After her death, the organization changed its name to the Satir Global Network. The organization's mission is to further healthy and just relationships in which people honor the self, other, and context. The Satir Global Network's aims are to provide an inclusive forum for the promotion of the Satir Growth Model, promote global networking, and transform systemic oppression and inequality. It provides education and training in the Satir Growth Model and helps further her ideas into the 21st century.

How Problems Get Solved

The Satir Growth Model is a strength-based approach, focusing on the existing resources that family members bring with them. Given that faulty coping strategies maintain problematic interactions, therapy provides a safe space for people to choose alternative ways of coping. Therapy helps increase people's self-esteem, leading them to be able to lean into their own uniqueness and providing a space for their loved ones to feel comfortable in their own uniqueness as well.

Whatever techniques the therapist uses, they are designed to help raise awareness within and between people in hopes of increasing self-esteem and self-worth so that people feel freer to be authentic—what Satir calls "congruence." Satir conceptualized a self-esteem maintenance kit, which could be metaphorical or literal. The kit is comprised of a detective hat, a medallion, a wand, a golden key, and a wisdom box. The detective hat is used when there is something new that the person wants to understand better. It helps them shift from judging an experience to exploring it. The medallion is two-sided and says "Yes" on one side and "No" on the other. It is intended to help the person recognize that they can say either word, depending on what they truly want, so they can maintain their integrity. The wand can be considered as a wishing wand, a courage stick, and an empowering wand. It helps people move from inaction based on fear to action based on desire. The golden key opens any door—helping the person ask questions they might not have previously, say the unsayable, and do the undoable. Lastly, the wisdom box helps connect the person to the wider world and all that has come before them. While the therapist is likely not to hand over these actual items, they will work with the client to utilize these new ways of being.

Family therapists operating from a Growth Model perspective are extremely interactive in the therapy room. Since making contact is such an important aspect of this approach, they try to use their whole self for contact. This includes adopting an **I-Thou perspective**, where they try to promote human-to-human interaction. Since one of the main goals of therapy is to help the client become congruent, it is important for the therapist to engage the client congruently. The therapist must be a real person who helps model a way of being for the client. Satir wanted therapists to try new ways of thinking and engaging in the therapy room, but to take and continue to use only those aspects that fit them. Given this, therapists believe in themselves as well as their clients. In many ways, the Satir therapist is like the humanistic therapist who believes that all people are constantly moving toward self-actualization—being the best version of themselves.

Different practitioners from this model may conceptualize therapy in different stages. However, they usually focus on a few main processes:

- the *status quo*, in which the family is currently and which is leading to difficulties;
- the *foreign element*—the family's expression of the desire to change;
- *chaos*—the therapist's introduction of novelty into the system;
- *integration*, where family members put what they learn from therapy into practice;
- *practice*, which involves trying out these learnings; and
- the *new status quo*, where a new homeostasis takes hold (Satir et al., 1991).

Throughout this process, the therapist raises the intensity of interactions so that people encounter their own experiences and can thus become more authentic (see Figure 6.6). Further, therapy then helps people to allow others to be more authentic.

Perhaps the most famous technique utilized by Satir is that of **sculpting**. In therapy, and in outside life, people learn to express themselves mainly through talking. If the other person does not understand your message, you must explain it in greater detail. When this happens repeatedly, others begin to filter out what we are trying to say, as they have already heard us say the same thing in the same way many times before. Sculpting helps people get in touch with

Figure 6.6 Satir's Growth Model can be seen as occurring through stages of therapy.

their inner experience and express this experience to others in a way that bypasses the typical spoken word.

Sculpting can be done in one of two primary ways. First, the client is asked to sculpt their family based on their experience of what it is like to be part of this family now. Second, the therapist can sculpt the family based on their own inner picture of the family's experience. Both methods are useful, since they attempt to connect the person to their internal experience.

Family members are asked to place other people in physical poses spatially located around the room and then to position themselves somewhere within this tableau. This is likely to have a visceral impact for each member of the family and may provide a new way of engaging self and other. This can then allow for new meanings to come forth, where people can become more authentically themselves. For instance, a daughter may position her father in the corner of the room, facing away from everyone, with his hands over his ears. The father may have never viewed himself as being distant and aloof. Being placed in this position by his daughter may act like a punch in the gut and make him reconsider what type of relationship he wants with his daughter and the rest of the family.

Typically, the therapist will begin with one member of the family. The choice of person will depend on the family organization, the presenting problem, and the therapeutic process. Once that person has presented their image of the family, the therapist acts as a guide for each family member, bringing forth their perceptions of this picture and what it represents about the various relationships in the family. The therapist then shifts to another family member to explore their experience, as every family member is unique and has their own way of seeing and being in the family.

Sculpting in this manner may be all that is necessary for people to explore themselves and seek a change in their relationships. However, therapists may also end the sculpt by having family members sculpt their desired picture of the family. This sculpt shifts the energy in the room from a focus on past problems and dysfunction to a future functional and supportive arrangement of relationships. In many of the desired sculpts I have done with families, their image usually depicts much closer proximity to one another, where they are touching one another (either holding hands or hugging). They also feel better about themselves and other family members. They can "feel" this both psychologically and physically.

Satir is also the family therapist who most utilized touch within her practice. Making contact is an extremely important concept within the Satir Growth Model. This contact comes into play through both an emotional and a physical aspect. Touch occurs between therapist and client as well as between clients. Satir viewed people as housing energy and as able to transfer this energy through physical connections with one another. The therapist may touch the client's hands, shoulder, head, knee, or other body parts. This touch helps connect the two and brings a heightened intensity to the contact. Between family members, touch—perhaps through holding one another's hand or giving a hug—shifts people from perhaps adversarial positions to understanding that they are connected to one another and have an influence on whether that contact goes positively or negatively.

From a Student's Perspective

Experiential family therapy is what I like to call the "get out of your seat and do something" therapy. The essence of experiential family therapy is in the name and learning about this model as a student was a physical, mental, and emotional experience. It is in stark contrast to our traditional notions of "talk therapy," where we envision a therapist and a client sitting facing one another and simply talking for an hour. When I use experiential family therapy with my clients, we are up out of our chairs, moving around the room, meditating, breathing, and reflecting on our emotions—we are engaging in activities that allow us to experience the self differently.

Kayleigh Sabo, doctoral student

Sculpting and touch are two specific techniques. A fuller intervention Satir therapists might use is **family reconstruction**. This intervention is designed to help an individual connect better to the historical and psychological interconnections of their family. By seeing self and family of origin with a new perspective, the individual might then feel more freedom to engage in new possibilities for the future.

Family reconstruction tended to occur during the many workshops that Satir conducted. It focuses primarily on the **star** (i.e., the person whose relationship with the family is being explored and worked on). The therapist prepares the reconstruction by talking with the star about their family history. This involves developing a **family map** (in essence, the primary family triad, although it could also include the grandparents); a **family life chronology** (highlighting three generations of the star's family, including important dates and historical events—similar in some ways to a genogram); and the **wheel of influence** (a chart including all the people who influenced the star when they were growing up).

In the workshop, the therapist recruits participants to play the various roles of people who were influential in the star's life. The therapist (also called the "guide") begins the family reconstruction by telling the star's story; then sculpts the family of origin, the star's parents' families of origin, and the star's parents' relationship; and then resculpts the star's family of origin. The overall goal is to increase the star's self-esteem so they are empowered to engage with themselves and others in new and more productive ways. This should engender more hope in them for their future.

Another primary technique Satir used is the **parts party**. Based on the notion that people have many faces—aspects of self—a parts party helps people to accept that they also have many possibilities. Some of our parts may be lying dormant, and when we access them, we increase our resources. The parts party helps people to acknowledge, accept, transform, and integrate their parts. Other workshop participants play the role of the various parts to help the person move from internal processes to more interpersonal processes.

SYMBOLIC-EXPERIENTIAL FAMILY THERAPY

Similar to Satir's Growth Model, **symbolic-experiential family therapy** attempts to free people from perceived restraints so they can be whole and fully functional. Carl Whitaker, the developer of the model, also sometimes called it a "therapy of the absurd." This is because Whitaker took the notion of absurdity to new places. For him, people limited themselves based on not accepting their full selves. **Absurdity** happens when people realize that what they have been thinking is not as fearful or destructive as they originally imagined. For instance, a husband who thinks he cannot have bad thoughts about his wife is engaging in absurdity. People make us angry—even those we love and are close to. We can't not have a bad thought about someone.

One of the difficulties of symbolic-experiential family therapy is that Whitaker was opposed to theory. In his view, if a theory became regimented, so did the therapist. This would be problematic because the therapist would be unable to be fully present and spontaneous, which is the goal for both family therapists and clients. If the model is manualized, or at least fairly structured, the therapist would double-think themselves and not allow their unconscious to help inform what they should do. Spontaneity is an extremely important ability for both therapist and client. The more people can allow themselves to be spontaneous, the more authentic they will likely be.

Major Players

Carl Whitaker (1912–1995) was born in upstate New York and grew up on a dairy farm. His family then moved to Syracuse, New York, where Whitaker went to high school. He stayed local and went to Syracuse University, where he eventually earned his M.D. in 1936. Whitaker first went into obstetrics and gynecology, but then switched to become a psychiatrist. During World War II, he worked in Oak Ridge, Tennessee (where a top-secret project developing the atomic bomb was located). When seeing patients, Whitaker was mainly self-taught. This led him to take on a co-therapist, which became a mainstay of his practice. In 1946, Whitaker was named chairman of the Department of Psychiatry at Emory University. In 1956, he and a few colleagues left Emory and opened the Atlanta Psychiatric Clinic, a private practice where his approach, **symbolic-experiential family therapy**, was further developed. In 1965, Whitaker moved back into academia, taking a position in the Department of Psychiatry at the University of Wisconsin. His most famous books include *The Family Crucible* and *Dancing with the Family*.

Why Families Have Problems

Families tend to have problems because they are engaging in rigid and repetitive ways of interacting. People have developed limiting roles, such as the black sheep or the dutiful wife. Operating only from this one role, people don't access all aspects of self. For instance, the dutiful wife cannot express anger. The black sheep cannot express helpfulness. The white knight cannot express mischievousness. However, people are not usually aware they are operating from such a limiting role. Further, they are not connected to their emotions and how they suppress them.

For Whitaker, this restriction of experiencing was considered crazy. **Craziness** can be viewed in two ways: one positive and one negative. Negative craziness happens when people restrict themselves to a rigid way of believing and doing. Most families that come to therapy have most, if not all, members acting crazy in this way, which can be seen in the variety of symptoms they experience. Negative craziness leads people to continue behaving in ways that are not working without being able to see new possibilities. Positive craziness occurs when people don't restrict themselves to rigid roles and rules. Rather, they can be spontaneous and allow themselves to experience the full possibilities of their being. This type of craziness leads to growth. Whitaker liked to say that he considered himself crazier than his clients, but that he made a living from it!

Symptoms happen in families when members develop expectations of themselves and others that are limiting. They've learned how to be with one another using fused or rigid boundaries. When there are fused boundaries, members become overly dependent on one another. They then are unable to assert their individuality. With rigid boundaries, members feel isolated from one another. Each extreme boundary limits people's expectations of self and others, where they are unable to access the full range of their experience.

These extreme boundaries get pushed further away from the center when the family experiences some type of stress. Some stress comes from outside of the system, such as from school, work, or social situations. Stress also happens when the family moves to a different development stage, such as the birth of a child or the launching of a child. If you are currently in college, think about what happened when you first started college. Were you allowed to go to a university away from home? How much freedom were you given? Were you still treated like a child or as an adult? Families might also have intergenerational stress, such as when adult children care for their ailing elderly parents. In all these situations, family members tighten up and try to become even more rigid in how they view themselves and others, as this is how they think they can better handle their problems. When they do so, they restrict the possible alternatives that could help the family to grow.

How Problems Get Solved

The goal of symbolic-experiential family therapy is about growth rather than symptom remission. Symptoms are a result of restrictions.

When the family grows through the development of autonomy in its members, individual symptoms are likely to recede. Thus, therapy attempts to enrich people's lives, pushing them to experience happiness, sadness, anger, jealousy, joy, and the full range of all human emotions. Therapy is not about education but rather about experiencing, helping people to move beyond arbitrarily placed limits on what they can think, say, or do.

The symbolic-experiential family therapist can be likened to a coach, but not a player on the team. They will challenge people to examine the interdynamics happening in the family, but family members always have free choice in what they do. In this vein, Whitaker discussed two types of battles that happen in therapy: the battle for structure and the battle for initiative.

In the **battle for structure**, there is a determination of what therapy will look like. In this battle, the therapist must win. Families come to therapy and try to recapitulate their interactional process, incorporating the therapist into it. However, it is exactly this process that is maintaining the problem and that needs to be altered. If the therapist capitulated to the family's demands, they would be reinforcing the dysfunctional family process. Thus, from the start of therapy, the therapist needs to send the message that something different will happen. As one example of the battle for structure, the therapist needs to determine who will come to sessions, since this signals that it is the whole family, rather than a single individual, that needs to change. At one point in his career, Whitaker would only work with a family if they brought four generations to sessions. This would be much more difficult to do today, given that people are having children later in life and have become more transitory: since the middle to late 20th century, people have become more mobile and have put down roots in locales that are far away from where they were born and raised.

In the **battle for initiative**, there is a determination of what family members will do in their lives (see Figure 6.7). This battle needs to be won by the family. Symbolic-experiential family therapists do not try to tell family members what to do or how to live their lives. If they did so, they would be discouraging family members from being authentic. The family must take the initiative in how they want their life to go, with the family members actively supporting this push.

Perhaps more than any other family therapy approach, symbolic-experiential family therapy attempts to shake up the family. Instead of trying to make family members feel better by comforting or reassuring them, the therapist probes for the unexplored areas of the family

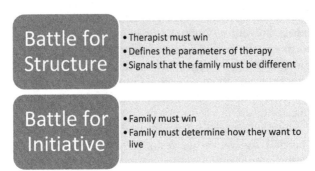

Figure 6.7 Symbolic experiential family therapy involves two battles: the battle for structure and the battle for initiative.

that are lurking underneath their interactions. They then bring these to the surface and let the family come to terms with them. In essence, the therapist increases the anxiety in the therapy room, so that the family's normal ways of dealing with stress don't relieve it. They will then need to develop new ways of being with one another.

Symbolic-experiential family therapy probably has the least formal techniques of any approach, save maybe Bowen therapy. However, this doesn't mean that the therapist doesn't have a lot of tools available to them. They have an unlimited amount. Anything can be used if it serves the purpose of helping people be more authentic. Whitaker was perhaps the most provocative of all family therapists, going beyond conventional ways of therapy. He was known at various points in his career to have adult clients sit on his lap and drink from a baby's bottle; fall asleep in session and wake up to explain a dream he had; or give a couple two batakas (foam bats) so they could hit each other over the head with them.

One of the hallmarks of this model is the use of a co-therapy team. The co-therapists are there to help augment each other. While one person is engaged with the family, the other can sit back and get a wider view of the family process. They can then put this information back into the conversation to try to stir up the family. Further, having co-therapists prevents one therapist from taking over the family. The co-therapists can model for the family how to engage one another productively, even if at times they disagree with one another.

Symbolic-experiential family therapists are likely not to engage in psychoeducation, as they believe it is experience rather than education that leads to change. Thus, the therapist's way of being in the room is intended to push people outside of their self-prescribed roles. When this happens, people need to find new ways of being that will help them deal with the current stress. There is no set point for termination, as the goal of therapy is growth rather than the achievement of a behavioral goal. Perhaps people will have a greater ability to be spontaneous when they finish therapy. They will be able to be connected as a unit while also maintaining a healthy level of autonomy.

GLOSSARY

- **Absurdity**: When people realize they are limiting themselves unnecessarily.
- **Battle for initiative**: A therapeutic process which the therapist attempts to get the family to win by having them decide how they want to live their life.
- **Battle for structure**: A therapeutic process which the therapist attempts to win by deciding how therapy will be organized.
- **Blaming**: A survival stance where a person discounts the other while privileging self.
- **Congruent**: The ideal communication stance, where a person is privileging self, other, and context.
- **Experiential family therapies**: A group of therapies that focus on helping people experience the here-and-now and being their authentic self.
- **Family life chronology**: An exploration of a person's family, usually entailing three generations (similar to a genogram).
- **Family reconstruction**: A therapeutic process that explores a person's family of origin and reenacts it within the session for the person to have a different current experience.
- **Irrelevant**: A survival stance where a person discounts self, other, and context.
- **Negative craziness**: When people act in ways that conform to limiting norms.
- **Parts party**: A therapeutic technique that gets people to enact aspects of a person's self so the person can engage those parts in the moment.
- **Placating**: A survival stance where a person discounts self and defers to someone else.
- **Positive craziness**: When people act in ways that do not limit themselves.

- **Sculpting**: A therapeutic technique that puts people into physical positions that represent what they are experiencing.
- **Self-mandala**: A concept whereby the person always has eight universal resources available to them.
- **Super-reasonable**: A survival stance where a person discounts self and other, but privileges the context.

CHAPTER SUMMARY

- Satir's Growth Model focuses on how people develop low self-esteem and use survival communication stances to try to cope.
- Congruent communication is an ideal, where people operate from high self-worth and self-esteem.
- The Satir Growth Model encourages people to be authentic while also appreciating other people's uniqueness.
- Symbolic-experiential family therapy holds that people tend to self-limit themselves, taking on a prescribed role and not fully experiencing themselves.
- Symbolic-experiential family therapists attempt to win the battle for structure, where they decide how therapy will be organized. However, they push the family to win the battle for initiative, where the family must decide how they are going to live their lives.
- The symbolic-experiential family therapist pushes self and family members out of prescribed roles so they move beyond their limiting ways of being.

REFERENCES

Napier, A.Y., & Whitaker, C.A. (1978). *The family crucible*. Harper & Row.

Satir, V. (1983). *Conjoint family therapy* (3rd ed.). Science and Behavior Books.

Whitaker, C. A., & Bumberry, W. M. (1988). *Dancing with the family*. Brunner/Mazel.

STRATEGIC FAMILY THERAPIES

ORIENTING QUESTIONS

- What are the main components that make an approach "strategic"?
- How does Mental Research Institute (MRI) brief therapy focus on failed solution attempts?
- What is the therapist's responsibility in strategic family therapy?

As we saw in Chapters 5 and 6, intergenerational and experiential family therapies are primarily focused on enhancing growth in families, regardless of the presenting problem. In this chapter, we cover the strategic family therapies, where the goal is symptom reduction or elimination. These models put a greater onus on the therapist to develop a pathway toward specific behavioral change. They are usually short term, symptom focused, and goal directed.

This chapter covers the strategic family therapies of MRI brief therapy and strategic therapy.

MRI BRIEF THERAPY

MRI brief therapy was born from the seminal work of Gregory Bateson and his research team exploring communication. Based on the tenets of cybernetics, general systems theory, and information theory, this group was one of the first to move toward short-term therapy. The model was developed in the 1960s and disseminated to the public in the 1970s. If you think back to the primary modality of that time, psychodynamic therapies were predominant. Patients

DOI: 10.4324/9781003312536-7

would go to therapy several times a week for several years. Thus, when the MRI group capped the number of sessions they could have with a client at 10, this was frowned upon. How could you get a lasting personality change if you meet only a handful of times with someone? However, the MRI group was not looking for deep-seated personality change, but rather symptom resolution. Let's explore how they did that.

Major Players

The MRI brief therapy approach was based on the interactional and communicational understandings of Gregory Bateson and the therapeutic strategies and interventions of Milton H. Erickson. Bateson was the head of the group, and studied and promoted how humans (and animals) operate through cybernetic principles. On his team were Jay Haley, John Weakland, and William Fry. Each person studied various aspects of communication in differing contexts. At one point, Haley and Weakland wanted to study communication in hypnosis. Bateson introduced them to Milton Erickson, whom he had previously consulted when he and his then wife, Margaret Mead, had conducted anthropological research in Bali and thought that Balinese dancers were in a trance. After the introduction, Haley and Weakland would frequently travel to Phoenix, Arizona where Erickson lived, to interview him and eventually learn therapy from him.

Bateson's group then received a grant to study schizophrenic communication. They recruited psychiatrist Don Jackson, since he was the only one of them who had experience working with schizophrenics. Eventually, Jackson developed the MRI, along with Virginia Satir and Jules Riskin. They soon brought on board John Weakland, Paul Watzlawick, Richard Fisch and Arthur Bodin, as well as Haley and Bateson. The model that was developed at the MRI was called "brief therapy," sometimes referred to as the "interactional view." This was one of the first short-term therapy approaches.

Don Jackson (1920–1968) earned his M.D. and became a psychiatrist, studying for four years under Harry Stack Sullivan. He joined the Bateson Group in 1953, when it began exploring schizophrenic communication. This led to his contributions and the publication of the article entitled "Towards a Theory of Schizophrenia." In 1958, Jackson founded the MRI in Palo Alto, California, and was its first director. With his colleagues, he helped develop one of the first family therapy theories, brief therapy. His most important book was *Pragmatics of Communication*.

Paul Watzlawick (1921–2007) was born in Austria and earned his Ph.D. in philosophy in 1949. He then studied at the Carl Jung Institute in Switzerland, eventually earning a degree in analytical psychology in 1954. In 1960, Don Jackson recruited Watzlawick to the MRI, where he became an integral proponent of the interactional view and then later the emerging philosophy of constructivism. His most influential books include *Pragmatics of Communication* and *Change: Principles of Problem Formation and Problem Resolution*.

John Weakland (1919–1995) was born in West Virginia and at the age of 16 entered Cornell University, where he earned his degree in chemical engineering. He happened to meet Gregory Bateson and enrolled at Columbia University to pursue anthropology. There, he worked with Margaret Mead and Ruth Benedict on their Cultures at a Distance project. Weakland was the first person Bateson invited to become part of the group to study communication, where he studied the hypnotic work of Milton H. Erickson. Weakland's most famous books include *Change: Principles of Problem Formation and Problem Resolution* and *The Tactics of Change*.

Why Families Have Problems

All people and all families have difficulties; this is just a part of life that cannot be helped. However, not all difficulties become problems. **Problems** arise when people try to solve normal life difficulties in ways that not only don't solve them, but actually make them worse (see Figure 7.1). Therefore, the informal catchphrase of MRI brief therapy is: "The solution is the problem." Try to think about how this might have happened in your life. Perhaps you started dating someone and you found them to be a little distant from you. To ensure that things were going well in the relationship, you stepped up your

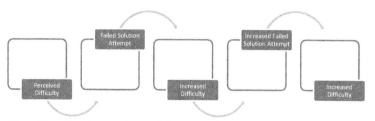

Figure 7.1 People experience difficulties when their attempts at a solution exacerbate the problem.

game, calling and texting them more, often asking them how things were in the relationship. For them, nothing had been an issue; rather, they tended to take things a little slower in developing a relationship. Things had been going fine, but your attempts to solve the problem by increasing your attentiveness to them actually scared them away. While you might not have experienced this exact scenario, you may well have experienced something similar that you can relate to.

Obviously, people don't intentionally attempt solutions that they think will fail. Based on their viewpoints, people attempt to solve problems the best way that they know how. Sometimes these attempts work. For instance, a daughter is acting out, so the parents take away her phone. She then behaves in the way that they prefer. This solution attempt has worked and thus there is no longer a problem. In therapy, you will meet families where these solution attempts have been unsuccessful.

The MRI theorists found that there are five basic attempted solutions to problems. First, people try to force something that can only occur spontaneously. This is usually when the person has a complaint about themselves. Think about when you can't fall asleep; the more you try to force yourself to go to sleep, the more you stay awake. Second, problems happen when people are fearful of an event, such as public speaking or performance, and try to postpone it. This only maintains the fear (and is one of the reasons why, if you are anxious about doing something, you should volunteer to go first, to get it over with!). Third, people try to make an àgreement with one another through opposition. Here, people try to solve a problem through competition rather than cooperation. This usually occurs when one party tries to demand actions from the other person, which leads to a one-up/one-down relationship. Fourth, people try to get others to go along with them through voluntarism. Instead of asking directly for what they want, people try to get the other person to want to do something even if they don't. In essence, the person thinks: "I want him to *want to* do it, not just because I am asking." Lastly, if someone is accusing you of something, you try to defend yourself.

One reason that many solution attempts fail is that people use first-order change attempts rather than second-order change attempts. Let's play a little game. Figure 7.2 presents the nine-dot problem. Here are the rules:

- You must connect all nine dots.
- You can only use four straight lines.

Figure 7.2 The nine-dot problem helps us to understand first-order and second-order change attempts.

- Once you put your pen down on the paper, you cannot lift it off.
- If you go back over a line, that counts as another line.

Take a moment and see if you can figure it out. Keep on reading, and we will get to the answer in a little bit.

How Problems Get Solved

If problems are maintained because of the family's failed solution attempts, one of the pathways toward change is to get people to stop trying to solve the problem in ways that have been ineffective. In essence, therapy is about getting clients to do something that is 180 degrees different than what they have tried in the past. MRI therapists explore what these failed solution attempts have in common. And likely, it is that they are all first-order change attempts. So, let's examine this concept, since it is very important for this model.

First-order change is change within the existing rule structure. In Chapter 3, we highlighted the notion that families maintain homeostasis, which is based on the rules of interaction between people. Growing up, your family probably had similar rules to many other families, which held that your parents were in charge and the children were supposed to listen to them. When you got in trouble (I know that you didn't, but let's just pretend for example's sake), your parents did things to let you know that you were misbehaving and that you should behave better. They may have had a talk with you, grounded you, given you extra chores, or taken away your iPhone. What do all these things have in common? What is the common theme? It is that the parents are in charge and should try to get the child to behave.

First-order change attempts are often effective. If your grades started to decline and your parents grounded you and your grades improved, great: their solution worked, and life is perfect! However, the families that wind up in family therapy aren't so lucky. Their first-order change attempts didn't work. Not only that, but they made things worse. Imagine that your grades are falling and your parents talk to you about it. This infuriates you, and you decide you're going to teach them a lesson that they don't control you. Your grades get worse, so they ground you. You then spend your days on the computer playing video games and giving them attitude. Now, not only are your grades not improving, but the relationship you had with your parents is getting worse. And like all problems, these issues are maintained by more-of-the-same solution attempts.

What is needed is **second-order change**: a change in the rules of the system. With this thought in mind, go back to the nine-dot problem and see if you can solve it now (if you didn't before). Were you successful? If not, go to the end of the chapter to see the solution. Many people are unable to solve the nine-dot problem because they add an additional rule that was never given to them. Based on Gestalt psychology, they view the nine dots in terms of a box and assume they have to stay within that box. If you do so, then yes, this puzzle is unsolvable. However, when you change the rules so you can go outside of the box, it is easily solved.

MRI therapists help clients to shift from first-order to second-order change techniques, changing the rules of the system. Now, the question arises: who needs to come to family therapy? How many members of the family are needed in session? The answer, as we know, is one. Since problems are maintained within the system, when one person in that system changes, they change the pattern. This leads to system-wide change. MRI therapists prefer to work with customers rather than **window shoppers** (i.e., people who come to therapy but do not really want change to happen). The **customers** are the family members who don't like something happening in the family and want to do something about it.

Interventions

MRI techniques and interventions are usually classified as being **paradoxical**. That is, they seem to be counterintuitive to what the client wants. People who are unfamiliar with these types of interventions might call them reverse psychology; however, they are a bit more than that. This section covers some of the primary MRI interventions.

When clients come in trying very hard to solve a problem but are unable to do so, MRI therapists tend to try to get them to **go slow**. The therapist will provide a rationale for why it makes sense for the client to go slow. "We want to make sure we understand exactly what's happening. It's like if your car intermittently made a noise, your mechanic might ask you to drive it around so that you could better explain the various details of when this is happening. So, for me to get a better sense of this problem, I want you to go slow. Don't try to change anything, but just keep note of it." This is a paradoxical directive, since the client is coming in wanting to change the problem and you are telling them not to change.

Another technique is called **benevolent sabotage**, which is usually used with parents who are having trouble with a teenager. If the teen is not cleaning their room and the fights have gotten worse, with the parents trying to get the youth to clean to no avail, the therapist might say: "Look, you've tried to reason with him and that didn't work. You've tried to punish him, and that didn't work. You've begged, pleaded, and bribed, and that didn't work. So, something different needs to happen. They are expecting you to be a competent adult. What I'd like you to try is to clean their room, but mess up somehow. Maybe this is by leaving crumbs in their bed or throwing away something they wanted. When they complain to you about it, apologize and say that you were trying to do a good job but have so much on your mind that you weren't yourself. Then see what happens." Unintentionally, my mother used benevolent sabotage when I was a pre-teen when she washed my whites with my colored clothes (particularly reds), and I ended up with pink clothes. I then quickly learned how to do my own laundry.

As explained, MRI therapy is about getting clients to do something 180 degrees different from the failed solution attempt. If you come to therapy because of a fear of public speaking, the therapist will explore with you how you've tried to solve the problem. Usually, you try to tell yourself not to be nervous and not to show nervousness to the audience. What is 180 degrees different? Having your first sentence to the audience be: "I am so nervous, I'm about to pee my pants" (or something like that). For a perfectionist, they might get the person to purposefully play a wrong note (if they are a musician) or incorrectly answer a question they know the answer to in an exam. Think about a current difficulty you are having and see what happens when you do something 180 degrees different from your past failed solution attempts!

From a Student's Perspective

To think systemically is to think in circularity. As a therapist, after learning about and trying to apply MRI brief therapy ideas, I am now looking for patterns in the system and avoiding my linear thinking. My ability to help the families differently started when I understood that if I continued implementing the same attempted solution that the families arrived with, I would fail them inside the therapy room. Understanding and implementing the fundamentals of MRI, which feeds other modalities, has enhanced my spontaneity and creativity in utilizing my clients' worldviews to their benefit. My integration into the system allows me to use interventions like therapeutic paradoxes, such as working with a child client that is afraid of the dark and prescribing him to interact with the darkness for a few minutes so he can blog his interactions.

Joseph Alvaro Guerrero, doctoral student

MRI therapy is known as brief therapy because the therapist contracts with the client for 10 sessions at most. If things get better in fewer sessions, the remaining sessions can be kept in the bank. But starting therapy with this expectation of only 10 sessions sets the stage for the client to expect quick change.

Termination happens in MRI brief therapy when the client says the concern that brought them to therapy is no longer a problem. Perhaps the problem is gone, or its intensity has reduced such that it is no longer problematic. The therapist takes the client's word on whether something is a problem. That is, if a family comes in saying they are concerned about the daughter sneaking out of the house, and at the end of therapy the daughter is no longer sneaking out, therapy has been successful. This is the case even if the spouses are arguing with one another about something else.

Fun Facts

The MRI, located in Palo Alto, California, is the birthplace of the interactional view and brief therapy, which gave birth to many of the other models of family therapy. It was founded in 1959 by Don Jackson, who brought on board Jules Riskin as Assistant Director and Virginia Satir as Director of Family Therapy Training. The MRI received funding from the National Institute of Mental Health and developed the first formal training program in family therapy. The MRI supports research exploring how people behave; provides training, consultation, and clinical services; and promotes new understandings of how to resolve human problems. Hundreds of books and articles were written based on the work done at the MRI. It is still active today.

STRATEGIC THERAPY

Strategic therapy was primarily developed by Jay Haley, beginning from his collaboration with Milton Erickson, the world-famous hypnotherapist. Haley incorporated Erickson's strategic techniques, Bateson's cybernetic ideas, and the hierarchical organization of families from structural family therapy, as he worked with Salvador Minuchin at the Philadelphia Child Guidance Clinic. There, Haley met **Cloé Madanes**, whom he married. They moved to Washington, D.C., and opened the Family Therapy Institute. Eventually, the two divorced. Madanes continued with her brand of strategic therapy, recently developing strategic coaching. Haley moved to La Jolla, California, married Madeleine Richeport (an anthropologist), and focused on training people in strategic therapy, which he renamed as directive family therapy.

Major Players

Milton H. Erickson (1901–1980) was a psychiatrist and hypnotherapist who influenced many models of family therapy, including strategic family therapy, MRI brief therapy, solution-focused brief therapy, and neuro-linguistic programming. Erickson had polio when he was 17 and through his recovery applied many principles of self-hypnosis. Erickson's techniques became hallmarks of not only his approach, but many other theories. His use of suggestions, directives, ordeals, and hypnosis were all housed within the notion of **utilization**—that clients have within them the necessary resources to help them change.

Jay Haley (1923–2007) joined Bateson on the early communications research project that the Bateson Group was exploring. In one of the original explorations, Haley researched communication and hypnosis. Haley consulted with Erickson and became one of the leading proponents of Erickson's style. Haley was one of the originators of the **MRI** and the **brief therapy** that came out of that. In 1962, he became the founding editor of the *Family Process* journal, one of the first and most important journals in the field. Haley then moved to Philadelphia to join Salvador Minuchin at the Philadelphia Child Guidance Clinic. In 1976, he founded the **Family Therapy Institute of Washington D.C.** with his wife, Cloé Madanes. Haley's approach to therapy came to be called strategic family therapy, of which Haley and Madanes were the key founders. Haley's influential books include *Directive Family Therapy* and *Problem-Solving Therapy*.

Cloé Madanes (1940–) was born in Buenos Aires, Argentina. She was a student of Milton Erickson and worked for a time at the Philadelphia Child Guidance Clinic, where she met and then married Jay Haley. Madanes introduced the concepts of pretend techniques, love, and violence into strategic therapy, and developed a procedure for working with families in which there was sexual abuse. After her divorce from Haley, Madanes collaborated with Tony Robbins to develop the field of strategic intervention, in which she is currently utilizing strategic principles to help people through coaching. Her most popular books include *Strategic Family Therapy* and *Behind the One Way Mirror*.

Why Families Have Problems

Strategic therapy views people in their primary social context: their family. They hypothesize that families develop problems during life stage transitions. These stages of family life include birth, infancy, childhood, school, adolescence, leaving home, becoming a parent, becoming a grandparent, and dealing with old age (see Figure 7.3). These problems (also viewed as symptoms) represent stage-of-life problems in that the family has not reorganized to effectively deal with the demands of the new life stage.

As most other family therapy approaches, strategic therapists view families as engaging in repeated patterns of interaction. These

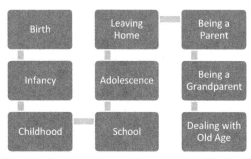

Figure 7.3 Strategic therapists pay attention to how families handle the typical life-stage transitions.

organizations include a hierarchy, which usually entails parents at the top and children at the bottom. Those families that have problems tend to (but don't always) have a problematic hierarchy, where there is a **cross-generational coalition**. A **coalition** occurs when there are two (or more) people who are united against a third. In your family, there would be a cross-generational coalition if you and one parent agreed to keep secrets from the other parent (e.g., "Don't tell dad, you know how crazy he gets").

Symptoms happen not on purpose but because of problems in the family organization. In a way, symptoms are useful and serve a function in the family. If your parents were having difficulties with one another but were unable to address them, you might unconsciously start to act out at home or school. Your parents would then focus their energies on you rather than each other. Thus, your symptom serves the family in a way.

Given that people engage in patterned behavior, strategic therapists look at the sequences of interaction between people. **Sequences** are the small bits of interaction that occur. For example, when you were 10, your parents probably told you it was time for bed. They would then (like I do with my son most nights) tell you to stop playing games on your iPad, go brush your teeth and get into bed. When this sequence happens on most nights, there is a pattern. And this pattern reinforces the hierarchy that the parents are above the child and have more power.

When Haley and Bateson were working together, they had a major disagreement about the notion of power. Bateson said that power did not exist, while Haley said it surely did. For Haley, **power** happens when one person's definition of the relationship takes hold.

If you've been in a romantic relationship or wanted one, you have firsthand experience of this. You are attracted to someone and must decide how you want to define the relationship: long-term romantic partner, casual dating, friends with benefits, friends, or no relationship (there are more choices between all of these). The other person is also trying to define the relationship based on what they want. If you want a romantic relationship, you will do things to get that definition to take hold: frequently text them, use cute emojis, talk about a future together ("What are *we* going to do this weekend?"), and perhaps send gifts, etc. If they only want a friendship, they will do things to define the relationship as such: not text often, not use cute emojis, talk about a separate future ("I'm hanging with friends this weekend. What are you going to do?"), and not flirt or send gifts. Whoever's definition takes hold has the power in the relationship. Usually, the person with the least investment has the most power. Problems tend to arise when people have different definitions of the relationship. Conversely, things work out more smoothly when both people are trying to define the relationship in the same way. Thus, it is better when you and the other person are trying to be just friends, or are both trying to be exclusive romantic partners.

How Problems Get Solved

Strategic therapy tends to be present and action oriented. Clients never need to know why a problem happened—that is, they do not need any insight. They just need to do something different. This push for change begins in the first session. Haley, when working at the Philadelphia Child Guidance Clinic, trained members of the community to become family therapists and developed a five-stage format for surviving the first session (see Figure 7.4).

In the **social stage**, the therapist makes a connection with every family member. They will likely ask children about school, hobbies, and friends. For adults, they might ask about work, hobbies, and favorite activities. Areas such as sports, movies, and interests are usually safe areas, where the therapist can begin to join with each person as well as the family as a unit.

During the **problem stage**, the therapist asks each person about what has brought them to therapy. Getting a clear definition of the problem helps the therapist learn how the family members think, which leads them to frame interventions in ways that make sense for the family.

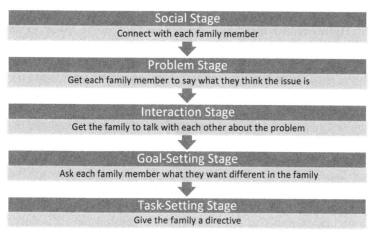

Figure 7.4   Haley developed a five-stage model for the first session.

In the **interaction stage**, the therapist will ask two or more family members to have a conversation about the problem. For instance, if the parents are complaining that the son is doing drugs, the therapist might say, "Talk with one another about this issue." As we will see in Chapter 8, this is a technique Haley borrowed from Minuchin, which is called enactment.

During the **goal-setting stage**, the therapist gets each person to describe how they want things to be. Since therapy is future focused and action oriented, the therapist wants to know where the family are going. While there may be differences between family members on the goals, the therapist will try to mutualize them. ("Mom mentioned son not doing drugs. Son mentioned mom and dad getting off his tail. Dad mentioned not fighting anymore. It sounds like you all want more peace in this family.")

Lastly, in the **task-setting stage**, the therapist develops an intervention for the family that is designed to move them one step closer to their goal. Strategic therapists take ownership of change. For them, if the family does not change, it is not because the family is being resistant, but because the therapist hasn't yet figured out the proper intervention. Strategic therapists call their interventions **directives**. Madanes (1991) once said that the directive is to strategic therapy as the interpretation is to psychoanalysis. It is the basic tool for the therapist to use. This next section describes some of the common types of strategic directives.

Strategic directives can be either straightforward or indirect. **Straightforward directives** are designed to get the client to do whatever is asked of them. If a youth is having trouble at school, the therapist might direct the parents to go to school with them and sit at the back of the class. If a couple is engaging in frequent fights, the therapist might direct them to write down their arguments to one another and exchange these notes, only having the argument through the written word. Whatever straightforward directive is given, the therapist wants the client to do that behavior.

Indirect directives are the reverse, where the therapist tries to get the client not to do what they say. These interventions are also known as **paradoxical techniques**. Strategic therapists tend to use indirect directives when there is a power struggle between therapist and client. Given that homeostasis is the combination of stability and change, paradoxical techniques focus primarily on the stability aspect. They are paradoxical because the client is coming to therapy saying they want to change. If the therapist thinks the client will try to counter any of their moves, they may use paradoxical techniques—suggesting that, at least for the time being, the client doesn't change. This then is a therapeutic paradox—which is a win-win, since if the client follows the therapist's directive and doesn't change, the therapeutic relationship is enhanced. If the client goes against the therapist, then they are changing, which is what they are coming to therapy for.

One of the strategic techniques that Haley borrowed from Erickson is that of ordeals. **Ordeals** are when the therapist creates a situation in which it is more problematic for the client to have the symptom than not to have it. Let's give you an example here to make things clearer. Suppose in a family the eight-year-old is wetting his bed. The therapist may then direct the parents to check the bed in the middle of the night. If it is wet, they must wake the boy up and help him practice his letters or numbers (or any area of schooling that he might be having trouble in) for some length of time (say one or two hours). The thought is that it would be too much trouble to have the symptom because if they did, they would have to do all this other stuff (the ordeal). But the ordeal must be good for the person (e.g., exercising, learning, etc.).

Madanes, among other things, added the intervention of **pretend techniques** to the strategic repertoire, which is based on the notion that symptoms are voluntary rather than involuntary. With the bed-wetter, strategic therapists think the person can control what they do. With the arguing couple, they can stop if they want. When utilizing pretend techniques, the therapist asks the family to pretend to have the symptom. Perhaps the family is coming because they say the teen is out of control. The therapist will ask the teen to pretend to be out of control and for the parent then to react to the youth. Family members will then not know whether the symptom is actually happening, or whether the person is only pretending it to happen. Further, if you can pretend it to happen, you can also get it not to happen.

Termination happens in strategic therapy when the family members are engaged in new sequences that better fit the current family life stage. These new behaviors are those preferred by the family and have happened repeatedly so that they become patterns of interaction. In essence, the family's homeostasis has changed.

In case you didn't figure out the nine-dot problem, here is the solution.

The nine-dot problem is solved when you shift from first to second-order change—changing the rules so that you can go outside of what looks like a box.

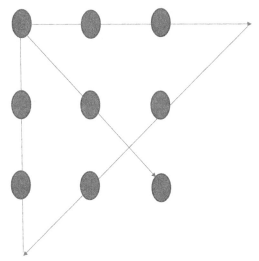

Figure 7.5   The nine-dot problem

GLOSSARY

- **Benevolent sabotage**: A technique whereby people attempt something but intentionally mess up to get the other person to become more competent.
- **Coalition**: When two or more people get together, usually at the exclusion of a third party.
- **Cross-generational coalition**: When two people from two different generations (e.g., parent and child; grandparent and grandchild) get together, usually at the exclusion of a third party.
- **Customers**: People who come to therapy wanting change.
- **Directives**: Strategic therapy's word for therapeutic techniques/interventions
- **First-order change**: Change (attempts) that happen within the existing rule structure.
- **Go slow**: A paradoxical technique telling clients to try not to change quickly.
- **Indirect directives**: Interventions where the therapist is anticipating the client challenging them and thus doing the opposite.
- **Ordeals**: Adding an activity the clients must do if they have the symptom, making having the symptom more problematic than not having it.
- **Paradoxical**: Interventions that focus on stability rather than change. Encouraging clients not to change when they are coming to therapy to change.
- **Power**: When someone's definition takes hold of the relationship.
- **Pretend techniques**: Getting clients to voluntarily pretend to have the symptom.
- **Second-order change**: Change (attempts) that change the rules of the system.
- **Sequences**: Interactions of behavior.
- **Straightforward directives**: Interventions where the therapist is trying to get the client to do what the therapist tells them to.
- **Window shoppers**: People who come to therapy but don't want change.

CHAPTER SUMMARY

- The MRI developed brief therapy, lasting for 10 sessions at most.
- MRI brief therapy takes the view that problems arise from people trying to solve normal life difficulties in ways that make the

problems worse. Thus, it is the failed solution attempts that are the problem.

- MRI brief therapy attempts to interrupt the failed solution attempts by getting clients to do something 180 degrees different.
- Strategic therapy is based on the strategic interventions of Milton Erickson, the cybernetic ideas of Gregory Bateson, and the hierarchical ideas of Salvador Minuchin.
- Strategic therapy views problems arising from people maintaining patterns of interaction that may have worked for a previous family life stage, but not the current one.
- Strategic therapy uses directives to get people to move incrementally toward their desired goals.

REFERENCES

Fisch, R., Weakland, J. H., & Segal, L. (1982). *The tactics of change*. Jossey-Bass.

Haley, J. (1987). *Problem-solving therapy* (2nd ed.). Jossey-Bass.

Haley, J., & Richeport-Haley, M. (2007). *Directive family therapy*. The Haworth Press.

Madanes, C. (1981). *Strategic family therapy*. Jossey-Bass.

Madanes, C. (1984). *Behind the one-way mirror*. Jossey-Bass.

Madanes, C. (1991). Strategic family therapy. In A. S. Gurman, & D. P. Kniskern (Eds.). *Handbook of family therapy: Volume II* (pp. 396–416). Brunner/Mazel.

Watzlawick, P., Bavelas, J. B., & Jackson, D. D. (1967). *Pragmatics of human communication*. Norton.

Watzlawick, P., Weakland, J., & Fisch, R. (1974). *Change: Principles of problem formation and problem resolution*. Norton.

SYSTEMIC FAMILY THERAPIES

ORIENTING QUESTIONS

- How do systemic family therapies conceptualize the current functioning of a family?
- How do Milan systemic family therapists incorporate hypothesizing, circularity, and neutrality into their therapeutic work?
- What usefulness is there in exploring a family's structure and how does that help structural family therapists to create hierarchical changes in a family?

Systemic family therapies focus on the overall functioning of the family, having space to understand multiple generations, but giving primacy to the nuclear family. Change happens by transforming the organization and patterned relationships between family members that maintain the problem. This chapter introduces you to Milan systemic family therapy and structural family therapy.

MILAN SYSTEMIC FAMILY THERAPY

Thus far in this book, we have introduced you to a variety of family therapy models. As you might have noticed, they all have their roots in North America. Milan systemic family therapy was the first foundational model of family therapy developed outside of the United States. However, it did so with roots in previously established models.

DOI: 10.4324/9781003312536-8

Major Players

Originally working with schizophrenics and anorexics using a psychoanalytic orientation, a group of Italian psychiatrists—Mara Selvini Palazzoli, Luigi Boscolo, Gianfranco Cecchin and Giuliana Prata—realized they were not achieving the success they were hoping for. They then focused on the cybernetic ideas of Gregory Bateson (specifically reading *Steps to an Ecology of Mind*) and frequently consulted with Paul Watzlawick, one of the developers of Mental Research Institute (MRI) brief therapy. They opened the Center for the Study of the Family in Milan, Italy and their approach came to be called Milan systemic family therapy.

The Milan Team (also called the Milan Associates) became recognized worldwide in the late 1970s, especially through their 1978 book, *Paradox and Counterparadox*, and their 1980 article, "Hypothesizing, Circularity, and Neutrality: Three Guidelines for the Conductor of the Session." The members of the team were as follows:

- **Mara Selvini Palazzoli** (1916–1999), whose most famous books include *Family Games* and *Self-Starvation*;
- **Luigi Boscolo** (1932–2015), whose most famous books were *Milan Systemic Family Therapy* and *The Times of Time*;
- **Gianfranco Cecchin** (1932–2004), whose most famous books were *Milan Systemic Family Therapy* and *Irreverence: A Strategy for Therapist's Survival*; and
- **Giuliana Prata** (1935–2022), whose most famous book is *A Systemic Harpoon into Family Games*.

In 1980, the team split: Palazzoli and Prata moved toward more strategic techniques, while Boscolo and Cechin developed the Milanese Centre of Family Therapy, where they promoted a more postmodern orientation.

Why Families Have Problems

Based on cybernetics concepts, the Milan Team viewed families as engaging in **family games**—the rules of interaction that perpetuate their current difficulties. These rules form the family's homeostasis. Since the family is a whole unit that has a corrective capacity that can lead to transformation, their current problematic homeostasis can be changed. Whereas MRI therapists would say, "The solution is the problem," Milan therapists would say, "The problem creates the system"—that is, the problem is not just housed within a few members, but within a larger system.

The Milan Team took great care to ensure that anyone associated with the problem was included in the treatment plan, including parents, children, grandparents, doctors, teachers, and other referring individuals. All these individuals are considered the **significant system**: the group of people and institutions that are attempting to solve the problem. A family's game incorporates various people into the rigid functioning of the family. Whereas families need to adapt and change over time, dysfunctional families maintain their homeostasis so they become frozen in time. Eventually, the family develops a way of viewing itself that is quite limiting. This **family myth** constrains members from behaving outside of their problem-maintaining rules.

While they may think they know what the problem is—namely, the identified patient doing bad things—they are unaware of the network of connections and beliefs around the problem that keep it part of their life. Milan therapy is thus about helping families to unstick themselves from the problematic family myth, shifting away from the destructive family games. The next section discusses how Milan therapists help families to change.

How Problems Get Solved

More than in any other approach, the Milan Team worked as a group. The four members worked in co-therapy teams, usually cross-gender. While one dyad worked with the family in the room, the other watched behind a one-way mirror. They then developed a five-stage session format (see Figure 8.1) that became a standard in most family therapy training programs. This format was used every time the family was seen. Milan-style therapy can be done by a solo therapist, but the idea is that the more people that can help develop a hypothesis and observe the therapeutic system interaction, the better.

Stage one is the **presession**, where the therapists get together and develop a hypothesis about what the family game is and their game plan for the session. The hypothesis is based on all the previous information they gathered. For the first session, this would include the intake or phone call information, as well as that from a referring agent if there was one. For all other sessions, the presession uses what occurred in past sessions to help orient the therapists to how they want to start the session.

The second stage is the **session**, which takes the bulk of the time with the family. Here, the therapists explore the family dynamics, teasing apart the family myths and the family game. One of the hallmarks of Milan therapy is the use of circular questions (which are described below). Family members are asked questions about the interactions of two or more other people in the hope of bringing difference into the conversation. This comes from the Batesonian notion that information is a difference that makes a difference.

After approximately 30 to 40 minutes, the therapists in the room pause and go behind the mirror to consult with the rest of the team. This **intersession** provides an opportunity for all the therapists involved in the case to talk to one another and update their initial systemic hypothesis based on the new information discussed in the session. You may be thinking to yourself that this would be very strange for the family members who are in the therapy room, but without a therapist at that moment. But throughout most of my own training, and most of my training of new therapists, I have used this process—what we call the consultation break. Most clients find that it is quite useful to the therapeutic process. They know there are people behind the mirror (ethically, you need to let them know, which is usually discussed in the informed consent), so this is just an expansion of the treatment team. Behind the mirror, the Milan therapists design an intervention that they think will help shift the family's homeostasis.

The therapist(s) then go back into the room and deliver the **intervention**. This is the shortest stage of the five: the idea is that the therapist goes into the room, provides the intervention, and immediately ends the session. If not, the family will have time to try to counter the therapist's attempts to change them.

The last part of the session occurs once the family leaves. The therapists have a **post-session** where they discuss how they think the delivery of the intervention went, further thoughts about the information that was discussed during the session, potential ideas for the next session, and a revision of the systemic hypothesis.

One interesting facet of the original Milan Team concerned the frequency of meetings with a family. Since they had learned about family therapy from the MRI brief therapy group, which had a 10-session limit, the Milan Team also used 10 sessions. However, this was over 40 years ago in Italy, when transportation was not as readily accessible or efficient as it is today; and families would have come to

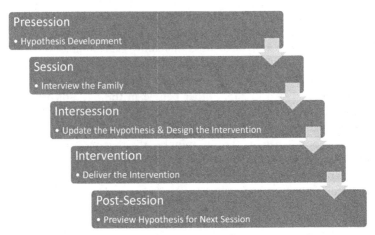

Figure 8.1 Milan therapists conduct sessions in five stages.

them from across the country. For some of these families, it may have taken a whole day to reach Milan. Given this, the team would tell these families to come back in a month's time. They found that the families who had sessions spaced one month apart experienced more rapid change. They then hypothesized that their interventions may need more time than just one week to be effective. Eventually, they spaced their sessions one month apart for all clients, while still maintaining the 10-session limit. Therefore, Milan therapy was referred to as "long-term brief therapy."

In 1980—the year the Milan Team split up—they also published one of the most influential articles in family therapy history, which discussed three guidelines for the therapist: hypothesizing, circularity, and neutrality. Let's take a few moments to go over each of these concepts, as they came to permeate the family therapy landscape during the 1980s.

The systemic hypothesis is the therapist's attempt to understand the functioning of the family and how they developed the family games and family myths that are maintaining their problems. **Hypothesizing** is a process the therapist engages in from the first contact with a client to the last. During sessions, the therapist asks questions based on their hypothesis, takes in information, adjusts the hypothesis, asks questions based on the new hypothesis, etc. (see Figure 8.2). It is important to remember that the therapist's hypothesis is never truth, but rather a successive approximation.

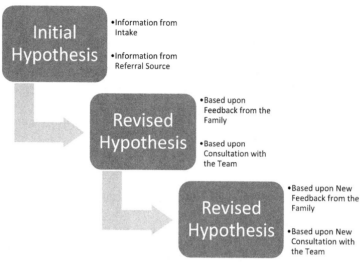

Figure 8.2 A Milan therapist constantly develops and revises their hypothesis about how the family is maintaining their problem.

The concept of circularity is based on Gregory Bateson's work in cybernetics that one part of the system cannot control the system. Rather, parts of a system mutually impact one another. In the therapeutic system, these parts include the therapist and clients. For Milan therapists, **circularity** entails conducting a session based on feedback from the family. This isn't necessarily the feedback we think about when we are getting constructive feedback. Instead, the feedback is information—specifically new information—about relationships, difference, and change.

The technique the Milan Team developed that has been most utilized by family therapists, regardless of model, is **circular questioning**—that is, asking questions that focus on the differences in perceptions of family members. Here are a few examples:

- "Who was the first to notice the problem?"
- "When mother becomes anxious, who does she turn to first?"
- "Who is son closest to? Mother or father?"

Each person is asked these questions so they can all see what each other thinks. What is likely to happen is that family members will hear someone else's perception that they didn't realize, which will be news to them and perhaps change how they then understand the family dynamics. After the Milan Team split, Boscolo and Cecchin moved almost exclusively to using circular questions as the primary interviewing and intervention modality of therapy.

The third guideline the Milan Team employed is **neutrality**, where the therapist attempts not to take any one person's viewpoint as truth. Each person is acknowledged when they talk but it is understood that this is their perception and not everyone else's. In session, a non-neutral stance can look like this:

> Therapist: What is happening in the family?
> Mother: My son is very disrespectful.
> Therapist [to son]: How come you are disrespectful?

In this instance, the therapist has joined with the mother and accepted her word as word. This likely will also lead to the therapist being incorporated into the family game and maintaining their homeostasis. A neutral therapist would have handled the situation in this way:

> Therapist: What is happening in the family?
> Mother: My son is disrespectful.
> Therapist [to son]: Your mom says you are disrespectful. How do you see it?

Here, the therapist acknowledges having heard the mother's statement and concern while also letting the son know that his position is equally important. This also becomes a starting point of setting the stage for differences to enter the therapeutic conversation. Therapeutic neutrality also occurs when the therapist is not wed to their hypothesis but is open to new information that informs and changes the current hypothesis.

Interventions

I want to go back to the intervention stage of the session, as we have described what it is, but not what happens in it. In this section, we discuss some of the famous Milan interventions. The original Milan Team, who were informed by strategic family therapies, observed that many families would come to therapy saying that they wanted change, but would try to maintain their stability by not following through with directives or by arguing against the therapist's position.

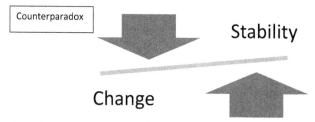

Figure 8.3 A counterparadox is an intervention that focuses on stability (no change) to get the family to change.

The Milan therapists viewed this as a paradox: "We want to change, but we will attempt not to change." In these cases, more-of-the-same solutions by the therapist would be attempting to get the family to change; the family would then try to maintain stability. The way out of this, for therapists, is to provide a **counterparadox**: an intervention that attempts to get the family not to change, but is likely to result in change (see Figure 8.3).

Like strategic therapists, the Milan Team would use prescriptions of restraint or engagement. **Prescriptions of restraint** are messages for the family to go slow and stop trying to solve the problem. The idea behind this is that the solution attempts are falling within the existing problematic family game. By having people stop trying to solve things, new ways of being with one another might develop. **Prescriptions of engagement** are designed to get the clients to engage in the problem. The family might be told, "Continue arguing like you are, since it will be useful for us to get a little more information on how this happens." Both interventions are paradoxical because the family is coming for change and the therapist is saying not to change (or even to engage more in the problem). If they follow the therapist's directive, it helps the therapeutic alliance as well as potentially bringing new information into the conversation. If they don't follow the therapist's directive, then they are changing.

Another significant Milan intervention is the use of rituals. **Rituals** are prescriptions given to families for them to engage in therapist-directed behavior in a consistent manner. The Milan Team's most famous ritual is the **odd days/even days ritual**, which is used with families where one or both parents are undermining the other when it comes to parenting issues. These families tend to come to therapy with one of the children designated as the identified patient. The therapist explains to the family that on odd days (Monday, Wednesday, and Friday), one of the parents is to have all parenting decisions. The other parent is not to be involved, even if the child attempts to triangulate them. On even days (Tuesday, Thursday, and Saturday), they switch roles. Sunday is up for grabs. As with most Milan techniques, the intent is to interrupt the family's game.

A related intervention, developed by Palazzoli after the split, is the **invariant prescription**. It is invariant because it does not change. She would give it to all families she worked with. Here, the parents are met by the therapist without the children. They are told that they should begin going out and not telling the children where they are going (obviously, they should get appropriate childcare). If the children ask them anything about the parents being away, the parents should tell them it is not their concern. This intervention breaks up the cross-generational coalitions that have previously developed.

The final Milan intervention we will talk about is the **positive connotation**, which is a specialized reframe. Here, the therapist talks about the symptoms in a positive way. Every family member's behavior around the symptom is talked about as being benevolent. In giving a positive connotation, the therapist might say:

> Your family is going through an interesting time. It's very nice that everyone is trying to pitch in to get you all through this. Janie's recent troubles in school have allowed you all to explore who you are as a family and make choices that solidify you as a family.

The positive connotation is designed to shift people's viewpoints of the identified patient and their behaviors from one of causing problems in the family to being useful to the family. With this reframe, the reactions to the behaviors might be different, which will then lead to difference in future interactions.

For Milan therapists, termination happens when the rules of the family game have changed. The family myth is switched so that people have new meanings for the relationships in the family and new ways of organizing themselves.

STRUCTURAL FAMILY THERAPY

Structural family therapy was developed by Salvador Minuchin and focuses on restructuring family organization so that more effective hierarchies are developed. Problems are viewed as occurring within the rules of interaction between subsystems and the boundaries between them.

Major Players

Salvador Minuchin (1921–2017) was born and raised in Argentina. Given his Jewish heritage, he experienced antisemitism and found himself needing to fight and challenge various systems. This comfort in discomfort would eventually play a significant role in the development of his therapeutic approach. Minuchin earned his medical degree and became a doctor in the Israeli army. He then moved to New York City and trained as a psychoanalyst. He was a child psychiatrist at the Wiltwyck School, where he and colleagues developed **structural family therapy**. In 1965, Minuchin became the director of the Philadelphia Child Guidance Clinic, developing it into one of the world's premier family therapy institutes. Minuchin was known for his ability to challenge families and systems to reorganize into more harmonious hierarchies. When Minuchin retired, he moved to New York City and established the Family Studies Institute. This organization was later renamed the **Minuchin Center for the Family**, which still provides training for the next generation of family therapists. His most influential books include *Families & Family Therapy* and *Family Therapy Techniques*.

Why Families Have Problems

Structural family therapy focuses on a family's current organization, especially relating to hierarchy. Families are composed of **subsystems**, while also being a subsystem of larger systems. The three primary subsystems in a family are the spousal, parental, and sibling subsystems. Subsystems may also form based upon gender, age, or interest (e.g., those who like art or athletics).

What distinguishes one subsystem from another are **boundaries**. There are three potential boundaries: diffuse, rigid, and clear (see Figure 8.4). **Diffuse boundaries** allow a lot of information to flow between people. If you and a parent talked to one another about each other's sex lives, filling them in every day on personal details, you likely had a diffuse boundary. **Rigid boundaries** are the opposite, as not much information flows between members. You had a rigid boundary with your parents if they had strict rules and were not open to hearing your thoughts on changing them. Instead, you likely heard, "I'm the parent and what I say goes." **Clear boundaries** are in the middle and allow information to flow, but at an appropriate level. If you had a curfew but were able to get it extended for an

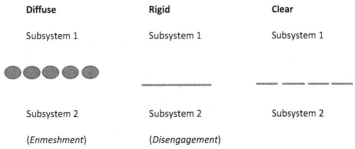

Diffuse	Rigid	Clear
Subsystem 1	Subsystem 1	Subsystem 1
Subsystem 2	Subsystem 2	Subsystem 2
(Enmeshment)	*(Disengagement)*	

Figure 8.4 There are three types of boundaries: diffuse, rigid, and clear.

event like prom, you probably had a clear boundary between yourself and your parents.

Each of these boundaries, at certain times, is functional. However, in most cases, clear boundaries are the most functional. Diffuse boundaries can lead to **enmeshment**, which is an overattachment between two people. Rigid boundaries can lead to **disengagement**, which is a lack of connection between people. There are times when people need more diffuse or rigid boundaries. For instance, families with very young children will likely function better when there are rigid boundaries. Imagine if, when you were three, you were able to set your own bedtimes, eating schedule, or what you were going to do all day. Chaos would have likely ensued. However, at your current age, having your parents dictate all the rules for you to follow would also lead to problems.

Structural family therapists hold that it is at family transition points that problems arise, since the family is still using an older organization to try to deal with the current situation. In essence, the family has not become adaptable. The family structure is stuck, and one (or more) member is experiencing symptoms that are outcomes of this no longer useful organization.

Fun Facts

Salvador Minuchin developed Family Studies Inc in 1981, which became a training and consultation institute. Here, Minuchin continued to train psychotherapists in the application of structural family therapy. He also engaged in consulting with larger institutions and systems, such as foster care agencies. Minuchin focused on working with marginalized families to help empower them, and did so by working not only with the families themselves, but the agencies that attempt to help them. When Minuchin retired, Family Studies Inc was renamed The Minuchin Center for the Family. Currently, the Minuchin Center trains psychotherapists in structural family therapy.

How Problems Get Solved

If it is the family organization and hierarchy that are problematic, then structural family therapists attempt to change the family's structure. This happens through various maneuvers to shift who is in which subsystem, boundary delineations, family hierarchy, and the rules of interaction between people.

Structural family therapists place strong importance on joining. **Joining** is more than a stage; it is a continual process. This is because challenge comes from connection. One of Minuchin's favorite techniques was the **stroke/kick**, where he would first stroke the family (e.g., "Wow, you all are very bright individuals") and then kick them (e.g., "So how is it that you do something that is so harmful to yourselves?"). This challenge is given to the full family rather than an individual and signifies the therapist's push that the family will need to change.

Joining also happens when the therapist adjusts themselves to connect better with the family. In **mimesis**, the therapist alters their mannerisms, such as their speech rate or mode of talking (e.g., speaking in metaphors if the family does), to match how the family communicates. This is one way that the therapist temporarily joins the family to create the therapeutic system. Another way is through **accommodation**: making small personal adjustments, such as taking off one's jacket or rolling up one's sleeves if the family's dress is more casual. Therapists also join through **tracking**, which involves listening to and acknowledging the family's story.

However, fairly quickly into therapy, structural family therapists attempt to change the family's story. Minuchin used to say that all families are wrong (Minuchin et al., 2021). This provocative statement implies they are wrong in that they think they know what the problem is (i.e., the identified patient), and they are wrong in that they think the therapist will do something about it. Early in therapy, and throughout the whole course of therapy, structural family therapists attempt to deconstruct the symptom. They try to shift the identified patient from whomever the family designates (usually a child) to relationships. Sometimes this happens through successive approximations, where the therapist may shift the identified patient from the adolescent to the mother to the father and then to the three-person interaction. Some structural therapists visualize this process through a **family map,** which is a depiction of the subsystems and boundaries in the family. The goal picture usually shows the parents at the top of the hierarchy with the children below and a clear boundary between them.

Perhaps the most famous of all structural family therapy techniques is the **enactment**, which is when the therapist gets the family to act in session like they do when they are at home. It gets the family to engage in their typical problematic patterns in the therapy room while the therapist is an observer (see Figure 8.5).

While enactments may spontaneously happen when family members begin to argue with one another in session, they usually happen when the therapist asks members to talk to one another:

> Daughter: My mother never listens to me!
> Therapist: Talk to her about that.

The therapist can then take a more distant position and observe the family's transactions. They can see what the rules are that the family operates from, the various roles that family members take with one another, and the organization. For instance, the above scene might continue:

> Daughter: Mom, you never listen.
> Mother: Yes, I do.
> Father: You just don't give your mother a chance.

Here, the therapist observes that there is a coalition of the parents against the child. They can then engage in **blocking**, where they stop one person from entering an interaction between other people.

Figure 8.5 Enactments allow the therapist to observe the family process by getting them to talk to one another.

Therapist: Father, hold on one second. Your wife and daughter were having a perfectly nice conversation and you came in to save your wife. She didn't need your saving right then. Could you sit back and just observe how they figure this out between themselves?

The therapist has shifted diffuse boundaries to become clearer to allow mother and daughter to engage one another in a new format.

Another structural technique is **boundary making**. What was just presented is an example of this and how a therapist can use an enactment not only to observe the family process and take in information, but also for interventive purposes. There are other ways of boundary making as well, where the therapist shifts the who and the how of the family's subsystems. Minuchin became famous for moving people's seating positions. He would ask a son who was sitting in between his parents to switch seats with one of them, so they could have an adult conversation. This maneuver helped strengthen the spousal and/or parental subsystem.

A related technique is **unbalancing**, where the therapist attempts to change the hierarchical arrangement of the family. Previously in this chapter, you learned about Milan therapy's position of neutrality. Unbalancing happens when the therapist is not neutral but rather joins one family member or one subsystem and not another. To unbalance the system, the therapist will temporarily take one side against another. For instance, a therapist might join with the wife and say to the spouse, "I feel for your wife. She is extremely overworked. She is doing so much. How can you help her?"

Structural family therapists try to get family members to become healers of one another. This then is a shift in roles, where the therapist unwraps the relational identities of the family members. It is based on the notion of **complementarity**: two people are viewed as yin and yang, and if one changes, the other will automatically change. An overworking wife is healed by a responsible husband. A father is labeled a sheriff and is healed by his children, who help educate him about the current generation. An overhelpful mother-in-law is healed by her daughter giving her permission to take a vacation from parenting.

From a Student's Perspective

When I first started learning and trying to apply structural ideas to my work, I needed a bit of a confidence boost, because you are telling this family you are working with, "You are doing things wrong; you are letting X family member guide the family"; and as a therapist, you are guiding them into an unfamiliar and more useful structure that they may disagree with. This can be about anything from changing who takes the lead in decision making to something as simple as who sits next to whom. It was a bit intimidating to do, I'm not going to lie. It was a style I wasn't too used to and stuff like the seat placement doesn't seem to say much; but it actually says a lot. It says who gets in the way of whom, who feels safe with whom, and who is the translator in communications between different family members; and you have to be willing to disrupt that for the sake of a healthier system for the family. It's also recognizing a lot of subtle and not-so-subtle cues from the children and parents—how, through action or inaction, one holds power over the other, and how that power may need to be overturned.

Luis Guerrero, doctoral student

Originally, structural family therapy focused primarily on the present, especially with the family process that was happening in the room. However, later iterations included a structural focus on the past (Minuchin et al., 2014). This new four-step structural model was used to guide the first few sessions of therapy (see Figure 8.6). Step one is when the therapist deconstructs the symptom. One of the first things the therapist does is to give the identified patient a voice. For instance, if the parents come in complaining about their teenager, the therapist quickly asks the teenager for their point of view. If the

Figure 8.6 One of the last iterations of structural family therapy included a four-step model of therapy.

parents talk about the child's incompetence, the therapist will ask the child about their competence. Deconstructing the symptom shifts the identified patient, which will be a process over the whole of therapy as families come in holding firm to what their view of the problem is. Sometimes this process is subtle. If a parent says their child doesn't listen to them, the therapist can respond, "Where did he learn that from?" This response shifts the problem from an intrapersonal issue (the child is defiant) to an interpersonal issue (they are only operating within an existing rule structure).

The second step is to explore the problem-maintaining family patterns. This is when the therapist will utilize tracking, enactments, and questioning of how the family members engage one another in ways that make them fall on their faces. The third step is new to the model (and is one that not all structural therapists utilize), where there is a focused exploration of the past. The therapist interviews one family member while the others observe and talk about how that person developed the lenses they are currently using. With an anxious parent, they might ask, "How did you learn that there is danger in proximity?" The last step is finding alternative ways of being. This is when the family members are challenged to function in new roles, with new subsystems, and with new boundaries.

Termination in structural therapy happens when the therapist has helped the family to reorganize so that their hierarchy and structure are more functional to their current life stage. The family came into therapy with a limited view of their roles and possibilities. Therapy helps let them know they are richer than they think they are, they have more available ways of being with one another and they can successfully manage their current family life stage.

GLOSSARY

- **Accommodation**: When the therapist makes small personal adjustments to better join with the family.
- **Boundaries**: The delineation points between different systems.
- **Boundary making**: Interventions that help shift who is in what subsystem and the boundaries between those subsystems.
- **Circularity**: Continuous feedback that occurs between people where they mutually influence one another.
- **Clear boundaries**: Boundaries where an adequate amount of information can go back and forth. In most cases, clear boundaries are the goal.

- **Complementarity**: The notion that two people are mutually influential to one another.
- **Counterparadox**: A therapeutic intervention that suggests the family not change in order for the family to change.
- **Diffuse boundaries**: Boundaries in which a lot of information can go back and forth. Diffuse boundaries can lead to enmeshment.
- **Enactment**: Getting two or more family members to interact with each other in session to bring forth their normal pattern of engagement.
- **Family game**: The rules of interaction in a family that perpetuate the problem.
- **Family myths**: The conceptualizations that a family develops about itself that keep the problematic family patterns intact.
- **Hypothesizing**: Therapists develop a relational conceptualization of why the family is interacting in its current way.
- **Invariant prescription**: A therapeutic intervention that doesn't change, regardless of the client, where the parents are told to go out and not tell the children where they are going or how it went. The intervention is designed to break up cross-generational coalitions.
- **Mimesis**: When the therapist alters their mannerisms to match the family's.
- **Neutrality**: Therapist position of not taking any one family member's viewpoints as truth.
- **Positive connotation**: A therapeutic reframe that highlights the positive aspects of family member behaviors around the problem.
- **Prescriptions of engagement**: Messages to the family for them to engage in the problem.
- **Prescriptions of restraint**: Messages to the family for them not to change.
- **Rigid boundaries**: Boundaries in which little information can go back and forth. Rigid boundaries lead to disengagement.
- **Rituals**: Prescriptions given to the family for them to do what the therapist says multiple times over the course of therapy.
- **Stroke/kick**: A therapeutic technique where the therapist first praises the family and then challenges them.
- **Subsystems**: Smaller units in a system.
- **Tracking**: When the therapist follows along with the family's story.

- **Unbalancing**: When the therapist temporarily takes one family member's side so they can change the boundary and subsystem configurations.

CHAPTER SUMMARY

- Milan systemic family therapy takes the view that problems arise in families because the family has adopted family myths that keeps problematic patterns (family game).
- The Milan Team developed a five-stage format for sessions that includes a presession, session, intersession, intervention, and postsession.
- The Milan Team developed three guidelines for therapists: hypothesizing, circularity, and neutrality. These guidelines inform their interactions with families and the design of their interventions.
- Structural family therapists explore the family's current organization, looking for areas in which the family has not adapted to their current life stage.
- Families organize based on various subsystems, which have various boundaries between them.
- Structural family therapists attempt to change who is in what subsystem as well as the boundaries between subsystems so that a more functional hierarchy is in place.

REFERENCES

Boscolo, L., & Bertrando, P. (1993). *The times of time*. Norton.

Boscolo, L., Cecchin, G., Hoffman, L., & Penn, P. (1987). *Milan systemic family therapy*. Basic Books.

Cecchin, G., Lane, G., & Ray, W. (1993). *Irreverence: A strategy for therapists' survival*. Routledge.

Minuchin, S. (2012). *Families and family therapy*. Routledge.

Minuchin, S., & Fishman, H. C. (1981). *Family therapy techniques*. Harvard University Press.

Minuchin, S., Reiter, M. D., & Borda, C. (2021). *The craft of family therapy* (2nd ed.). Routledge.

Prata, G. (1990). *A systemic harpoon into family games*. Routledge.

Selvini Palazzoli, M. (1977). *Self-starvation: From individual to family therapy in the treatment of anorexia nervosa*. Jason Aronson.

Selvini Palazzoli, M., Boscolo, L., Cecchin, G., & Prata, G. (1978). *Paradox and counterparadox*. Jason Aronson.

Selvini Palazzoli, M., Boscolo, L., Cecchin, G., & Prata, G. (1978). A ritualized prescription in family therapy: Odd days and even days. *Journal of Marriage and Family Counseling, 4*, 3–8.

Selvini Palazzoli, M., Boscolo, L., Cecchin, G., & Prata, G. (1980). Hypothesizing—circularity—neutrality: Three guidelines for the conductor of the session, *Family Process, 19* (1), 3–12.

Selvini Palazzoli, M., Cirillo, S., Selvini, M., & Sorrentino, A. M. (1989). *Family games.* Norton.

POSTMODERN FAMILY THERAPIES

ORIENTING QUESTIONS

- How does a focus on language make postmodern therapies unique from the other models of family therapy?
- How does solution-focused brief therapy (SFBT) help clients shift from the past to the present to the future?
- What are the implications of narrative therapy's deconstruction of the dominant narrative and highlighting of alternative plotlines?

Postmodern therapies highlight the understanding that there is no absolute truth. Rather, meaning is developed through language. Here, the therapist views the client as being the expert on how they make sense of their experience. Postmodern therapists don't view clients as being problematic or tell them what to do. Rather, clients are viewed as the experts on what they want in their lives, and the therapist is viewed as an expert in having a conversation that brings the client's expertise to the surface. This chapter covers two of the most significant postmodern therapies: SFBT and narrative therapy.

SOLUTION-FOCUSED BRIEF THERAPY

SFBT was developed by Steve de Shazer and Insoo Kim Berg in Milwaukee, Wisconsin. This husband-and-wife team had their roots in Mental Research Institute (MRI) brief therapy as well as Ericksonian hypnosis. Whereas MRI brief therapy explores the

DOI: 10.4324/9781003312536-9

family's failed solution attempts, SFBT highlights the family's past successes.

Major Players

Steve de Shazer (1940–2005) and **Insoo Kim Berg** (1934–2007) were the co-originators of **SFBT**. de Shazer was born in Milwaukee, Wisconsin, and was initially a musician, receiving a bachelor of fine arts degree from the University of Wisconsin-Milwaukee; he then earned a master's in social work from the same university. de Shazer was originally a practitioner of MRI brief therapy and Ericksonian hypnotherapy. He was good friends with John Weakland (one of the developers of MRI brief therapy), who introduced him to Insoo Kim Berg in the mid-1970s at the MRI, where she was studying their brand of therapy. Berg was born in Seoul, Korea. In 1960, she earned bachelor's and master's degrees in social work from the University of Wisconsin-Milwaukee. She then completed postgraduate training at the Family Institute of Chicago, the Menninger Foundation, and the MRI. de Shazer and Berg married in 1977 and co-founded the **Brief Family Therapy Center** in Milwaukee, Wisconsin in 1978. Instead of focusing on how problems develop and are maintained, they focused on what people were already doing that was useful and was working for them. de Shazer's most influential books include *Keys to Solution in Brief Therapy* and *Patterns of Brief Family Therapy*. Berg's most influential books include *Family Based Services* and *Interviewing for Solutions*.

Why Families Have Problems

Like MRI brief therapy, SFBT holds that people have problems because they engage in more-of-the-same behaviors. If you and your partner are having difficulties but neither brings this up, you each are holding it in and building up resentment. Not addressing the issue keeps the problem present and lets it fester. Further, when thinking about the situation, you likely keep focusing on what is not working.

Take a second and think about what you would tell a therapist if you were to go see one for a first session. You would likely focus on all the things happening in your life that you don't like, want less of, or don't want anymore. SFBT therapists call this **problem talk**. The more we keep problems in the foreground, the bigger they become. Thus, therapy is about getting clients to move away from problem talk and shifting their problems from the foreground to the background. The question then arises: what takes their place in the foreground?

How Problems Get Solved

SFBT therapists believe people already come to therapy with all their strengths, resources, and solutions to their problems. We don't need to teach them anything. Rather, we need to help them access what they already know that is useful for them. This is what is known as **solution talk**. In theory, we never need to talk with the client about their concerns or what they think the problem is, because the problem is not necessarily related to the solution. The therapist still usually spends some time listening closely to client concerns, but with an ear toward what has worked (see Figure 9.1).

SFBT therapists adopted from MRI three general rules for human behavior (see Figure 9.2). First, if it ain't broke, don't fix it. Sometimes you might have a relationship that is perfectly fine but for some reason, you think you need to change it. This change may actually make the relationship worse. The second rule is: if it doesn't work, don't do it again; do something different. This rule goes against the American adage, "If at first you don't succeed, try and try again." I had a cat who loved to be on the patio but only when the sliding glass door was

Figure 9.1 Solution-focused therapists help clients move from problem talk (i.e., talk of what is not working) to solution talk (i.e., talk of what has worked), and get them to do more of what has worked for them in the past.

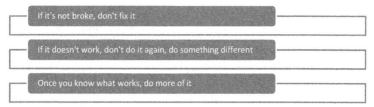

Figure 9.2 SFBT is predicated on three simple but complex rules.

open. One time the door got closed and the cat freaked out. He ran straight for the door and slammed headfirst into it. That didn't get him in, so he tried again by running back farther and then running faster toward the glass. Luckily, I was a little faster and got to the door first. This was literally banging one's head into a door doing the same thing over and over. It is the first part of this rule that most people utilize which leads them to therapy. They are doing more-of-the-same behavior. SFBT is designed to get them to do something different, which leads us to the third rule: once you know what works, do more of it.

So, what has worked for people? People do not experience their problems 24/7. There are times when the problem is not there, or not at the level that it currently is. These are known as **exceptions**: times when the problem could have happened, but did not. Therapy then becomes a process of bringing these exceptions to awareness and helping the client figure out how to make them more accessible. The SFBT therapist will **compliment** the client when they do something that is useful for them, helping to reinforce their positive actions. "Wow—how did you know to give yourself some space, as that was very useful for you?"

How do SFBT therapists engage in this solution-building process? They do so primarily through questions (see Figure 9.3). Instead of telling clients what is wrong with them and what they should do, the therapeutic process is a back-and-forth in which the therapist leads from **one step behind**, encouraging the client to do more-of-the-same behaviors that were useful in the past and that may be useful once again.

The expectation that clients come to therapy with strengths and resources can be seen in perhaps the first question the SFBT therapist asks clients: "From the time you made the appointment to come here, what has been different and better?" This **presession change question** sets the stage that therapy will focus on exploring what has been working for clients. Further, it demonstrates that clients have personal agency: they have already made positive changes without the therapist's help. While the therapist will be useful to help increase these and other positive client actions, it is the client that initiated and followed through on them.

There are times when clients talk in abstract ways. Therapists can help them be more concrete using **scaling questions**. You've experienced a scaling question if you've gone to the emergency room and the intake nurse has asked you to rate the severity of your pain on a scale from 1 to 10. Therapeutic scaling questions are the same, usually scaling what clients want (e.g., hope, motivation, peace, happiness). You can also use the same scaling question over the course of therapy, since the client's first answer is the baseline and their subsequent answers let you know whether change has happened. You can also ask about goals by moving up the scale. "You're at a 5 right now for happiness. When you are at a 5.1, what will be different in your life?"

Perhaps the most famous SFBT question is the **miracle question**. Here, the therapist presupposes that the problem is gone and explores what the client is doing, as these will become the goals for therapy. The miracle question goes something like this:

> Suppose tonight, when you go to sleep, a miracle happens. And the miracle is that all the concerns that brought you here to therapy [snaps fingers] are gone. However, you were sleeping when this miracle happened. So, when you wake up tomorrow morning, what will be the first thing that you will notice that will let you know the miracle has happened?

The answer to this question then becomes the focus of the conversation, to see how this has happened in the past and how the client can get it to happen again. To get the most out of the miracle question, you should use every therapist's best friend—the **what else question**: "Okay—so you would wake up and exercise right away. What else would you notice?"

As you might be thinking, SFBT is a very positive approach. And sometimes it can come across as too positive, with the therapist only wanting to hear about the good things happening in the client's life. When this happens, it becomes **solution-forced therapy**, which can be problematic. If you remember the second rule of SFBT—if it's not working, don't do it again—SFBT therapists can explore what hasn't worked. This is perfectly fine. You are just not going to spend session after session talking about what people don't want. At some point, the problem talk needs to switch to solution talk. One subtle way to do this, especially with clients who are having an extremely hard time, is by using **coping questions**. These questions acknowledge the current difficulty and try to elucidate the small and large things clients have done to ensure things do not get worse. "Wow—things are not going well for you now. With the illness and the losses, that is a lot to handle. What have you done so that things don't get even worse?"

You've seen that SFBT therapists focus on difference, with a preference for a positive difference. They do this through **what's better questions**. The presession question is the first that's used in the therapeutic process. However, second and subsequent sessions will usually begin with these questions. Many other therapists start sessions with what seems like a throwaway question: "How was your week?" This opens the conversational field to what went well, and—more likely—what did not go well. What's better questions use **presupposition** to expect that positive change has happened for the client.

Change happens when clients start to shift the lenses that they wear—from lenses that first see problems to lenses that first see solutions. Then they can do more-of-the-same as positive changes begin to snowball. While a lot of this lens shifting happens in session through the questions we've just discussed, long-lasting change occurs when people behave differently outside of the therapy session. SFBT therapists sometimes try to get this to happen by giving homework assignments (sometimes also called experiments).

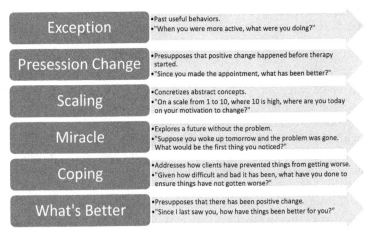

Figure 9.3 SFBT therapists primarily use questions as their interventions.

From a Student's Perspective

When I started learning the SFBT approach, the structuring of the questions in my mind was overwhelming. It was a *new language* I needed to learn because the idea that *clients already possess all the resources they need* was new to me. In psychology, we learn how people struggle with a specific problem. In the solution-focused approach, we turn our lens to what is already working in clients' lives and guide them to use those resources to move forward. I remember working with a high-school student who was suspended for getting involved in a fight to protect his little brother. I started the conversation by asking him about his best hopes from our conversation. The client talked about his dreams of working in UNICEF as a cultural ambassador and the skills he uses to gather the family together and help his immigrant parents to navigate a system they are not familiar with. Our conversation helped him gain perspective on his abilities and guided him to utilize them toward his desired outcome. Once I got the essence of asking questions from a solution-focused lens, our interaction turned into a natural and motivating conversation.

Elvan Okaygun, master's student

SFBT has developed interventions that are used for many people. These are called **skeleton keys**, as they open doors for a variety of clients. They include a **structured fight task**, where conflicting couples flip a coin and the winner gets to complain to the other person for 15 minutes, after which they switch and the second person complains to the first for another 15 minutes. If necessary, they then repeat the process. Another skeleton key is the **write, read, and burn task**, which is usually given to someone who keeps perseverating on a topic. They are told to write about whatever they are thinking about and can't let go of, to read the letter to themselves, and then to burn it once they have finished. Another skeleton key is the **do something different task**, where the therapist tells the client that the next time the problem starts, they are to do something—anything—that is different from how they previously tried to solve the problem. As you can see, what all these interventions have in common is that they interrupt the problematic pattern and switch away from the previous failed solution attempt.

However, the most famous skeleton key is the **first session formula task**. As you can guess, this task is given at the end of the first session and goes like this: "Between now and next time we meet,

I want you to pay attention to, and perhaps even write down, all the things that have happened that you want to continue to happen or to happen more frequently." Normally, people will spend the week nitpicking and paying attention to everything the others are doing that they don't like, so they can bring this up in therapy. Can you just imagine what it would be like to live with someone who was always on alert to every little thing that annoyed them? You would feel that tension and things would only get worse. The first session formula task changes people's lenses and gets them to pay attention to those occurrences they appreciate, which will lead them to interact better with others, which in turn will lead others to interact better with them, etc. Those aspects they notice that they would like to continue then become the solutions to be enhanced.

SFBT therapists view clients differently depending on their motivation for change (see Figure 9.4). There are some people who come to therapy at the behest of someone else. Perhaps the court has mandated therapy; or a parent is bringing in a child and the child doesn't think there are any issues. These individuals are called **visitors**, since they do not perceive that there's a problem and they don't want to try to change. Other people see there is a problem but think someone else needs to change to fix it. These individuals are called **complainants**. This is the parent in the previous example, who thinks their child must change for things to get better. Lastly, **customers** are individuals who perceive a problem and think if they make changes, things will get better. You can obviously see that we all want to work with customers. The question is how to get visitors to become complainants and then customers. For the visitor, the SFBT therapist may not ask anything of them or perhaps get them to think about what is happening in the hope they see that there is a problem. Complainants

Figure 9.4 SFBT therapists view clients differently based on their understanding of a problem and their motivation for change.

may be asked to observe interactions to potentially see that they have a role in influencing what happens. When working with customers, the therapist will ask them to do something, as they have the most motivation in attempting to change.

SFBT therapists view therapy as successful when the client states that the problem is no longer present or has reduced to the point where it is no longer problematic for them. This doesn't mean that problems won't arise in the future; but the client has now begun to utilize their strengths and resources to help them better navigate their current situation. Part of how they determine this is through the development of goals that are small, measurable, realistic, client desired, reflective of the client's hard work, and characterized by the presence (rather than absence) of something (see Figure 9.5). SFBT helps clients develop goals that fit all these components so that everyone knows when therapy has been successful. An example of this type of goal would be: "As a family, we will spend two hours together on Friday night playing games." It is small (only two hours), measurable (have they spent those two hours together?), realistic (not expecting them to get along every minute of every day), client desired (they want to be happy together), reflective of the clients' hard work (they are each engaging in it), and characterized by the presence of something (they are having game night rather than not fighting).

Figure 9.5   SFBT therapists help their clients to develop useful goals.

Fun Facts

Out of all the foundational family therapy approaches, SFBT has done the best job of supporting its effectiveness through research. Many studies have focused on the empirical validation (see Chapter 11) of this model. This is important in today's managed care environment, where insurance companies might only reimburse for treatments that have been shown to be clinically effective. In 2002, de Shazer, Berg, and colleagues developed the Solution-Focused Brief Therapy Association, which is still quite active today, hosting an annual conference and developing a treatment manual for SFBT. Visit sfbta.org to learn more about this organization and the promotion of SFBT.

NARRATIVE THERAPY

So far, you've seen that almost every foundational family therapy theory was developed in the United States, except for Milan systemic family therapy. We now take a trip to the other side of the globe, to Australia and New Zealand, where **narrative therapy** was initially developed by Michael White and David Epston. Narrative therapy shifts the focus of dynamics from the nuclear family to societal practices, particularly around power.

Major Players

Michael White (1948–2008) was born in Adelaide, South Australia. In 1979, he earned an undergraduate degree in social work from the University of South Australia. In 1983, he developed the Dulwich Centre, which is still operating today and is the premier training community for narrative therapists. Originally basing his philosophical underpinnings on the cybernetic work of Bateson, White connected with his New Zealand colleague, **David Epston**, and developed **narrative therapy**. They built their model on a wide range of fields, including literary theory, cultural anthropology, critical philosophy, and cognitive theory. Their approach helps people to separate themselves from the problems and reauthor the dominant stories of their lives. White and Epston co-authored the most influential book in narrative therapy, called *Narrative Means to Therapeutic Ends*. Just before his untimely death, White wrote *Maps of Narrative Practice*.

Why Families Have Problems

People story their lives—that is, they view their lives chronologically and highlight certain events to create an overarching narrative or story. Take a second and think about your life. If you were to give your life a story title, what would it be? Based on that title, what were the events that led you to call it that? What identity did you develop around that title? Where did you learn to view yourself in this way? Is this the story that you want for your life? These are the types of questions that narrative therapy tackles.

Narrative therapists explore two landscapes: action and identity. The **landscape of action** is the events that happen—for example, your parents divorcing; getting into trouble at school; winning $5,000 on the lottery; or ending a relationship with your partner (there are millions of potential entries into the landscape of action, but you likely only notate the most significant ones). The **landscape of identity** is how you view yourself based on what happened. Perhaps after your parents' divorce, you viewed yourself as broken; or after your relationship ended, you viewed yourself as unlovable.

These landscapes are connected to larger **dominant discourses** around who people are. As a society, what do we tell ourselves about relationships and what it means to be in love? There is a push for people to fall in love and be together. We've developed holidays around it (i.e., Valentine's Day) and have countless movies and novels about falling in love. There are social discourses on what it means to be a man or a woman (and lately new narratives about being nonbinary); to be young or old; to be Jewish, Christian, or Muslim; to be American, British, or Indian. What happens is that people internalize these larger systems' beliefs and self-police themselves. Take a young boy who might want to play with dolls but says to himself, "I can't because they are for girls"; or a woman who wants to have time away from her children but says to herself, "I can't because 'good mothers' always want to be around their children."

Families also internalize these stories, allowing the dominant knowledge—which they take as truth—to take precedence over their **local knowledge**, and what they want and prefer in their lives. Problems then develop and take on a life of their own, as family members act in ways that provide a **life support system for the problem**. When this happens, people begin living these **problem-saturated stories**. Narrative therapy focuses on helping families move from their internalized problem-saturated stories to bring forth alternative plotlines (see Figure 9.6).

Figure 9.6 Narrative therapists help families shift from problem-saturated stories to highlight alternative plotlines.

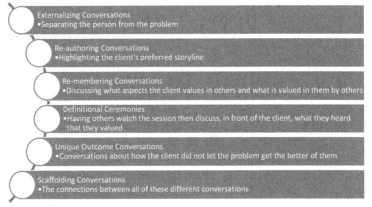

Figure 9.7 Narrative therapists might utilize various maps of conversations.

How Problems Get Solved

Narrative therapists help families to deconstruct the problem story and bring to the forefront their preferred ways of being. This occurs through a narrative conversation that can be viewed as a map to navigate the therapeutic landscape (see Figure 9.7). The map contains externalizing conversations, re-authoring conversations, re-membering conversations, definitional ceremonies, unique outcome conversations, and scaffolding conversations (White, 2007). This section discusses each of these types of conversations.

What has become the most famous aspect of narrative therapy is **externalizing conversations**, where the problem is considered as separate from the person. Like the notion of deconstructing the symptom so that it is not the identified patient that is the problem, narrative therapists shift the issue to the relationship between the person/family and wider society. This happens by talking about the problem as another entity. Usually, the client is asked what they would call the problem, how the problem has impacted them and what it has brought to their life. "How long has the Blue Depression been in your life?" "When the Nasty Rage makes a visit, what does it get you to do that you normally wouldn't?" This is why the slogan that has been developed for narrative therapy is, "The problem is the problem."

Externalizing the problem shifts the person's/family's identity from being the problem to being the victim (in the moment) of the problem. Therapy then attempts to increase their **personal agency** so they can become victorious over the problem. Further, therapy isn't necessarily about removing the problem from the client's life. Problems aren't totally problematic for people—for example, axiety gives people a chance to think a bit more and depression suggests to people to think about what they want in life. Narrative therapy helps people to think about what type of relationship they want with the problem and to have more ownership over that relationship, rather than letting the problem overwhelm and totalize them.

Re-authoring conversations provide an opening to shift from problem-saturated stories to alternative plotlines where clients have a greater sense of personal agency. What has likely been highlighted by clients are the feelings, events, and relationships that surround the problem. For instance, they focus mainly on arguments between spouses, thinking over and over about their anger toward one another and how the other person has wronged them. Re-authoring conversations explore the neglected areas of people's lives, bringing into focus people's caring for one another and ways they've tried to be loving to one another.

Re-membering conversations help connect people to self and each other. This comes through bringing to the surface people's desired identities. This can happen with family members where there has been a cutoff or even if they have passed away. "What did your father, when he was alive, value in you?" "What do you think your aunt would say about you and how you haven't let Worry dominate your life?"

Definitional ceremonies help expand the readership of the client's new preferred story. They happen when other people are invited into the session to discuss their experience of listening to the therapeutic talk. This can happen when other therapists watch the session and then conduct a **reflecting team**; or when past clients who have previously had success dealing with the problem engage in an **outsider witness** group. With either format, the clients must give consent to others viewing the session. Then the therapist and clients listen to the other group talk about what they heard in the session. After 10 to 15 minutes, the groups switch, and the clients and therapist discuss what they paid attention to in the talk from the definitional ceremony.

Unique outcome conversations happen when the therapist interviews the client about times and ways that the client did not let the problem dominate their life. This is like SFBT's exploration of exceptions. The focus is on highlighting how the client took personal agency and initiative to live their life in a preferred manner. "When have been times that the Blue Depression tried to come into your life and you said, 'No thank you'? How were you able to do that? What does that tell you about yourself that you were able to stand up for yourself at that moment?"

Scaffolding conversations bring everything together where, in small steps, the therapist walks with the client, uncovering how they have been living their life in more desired ways. These conversations move people from what is known and familiar (their problem-saturated story) to alternatives that have more possibilities. They shift clients' identities from being victims to heroes and demonstrate people's abilities for personal agency.

Throughout the therapeutic process, narrative therapists might utilize the written word to help bring forth this alternative knowledge. Many people have things written about them that are problematic. For instance, a troubled teen may have various documents about school suspensions, court transcripts, and psychological reports. These documents are likely to paint a picture of the person as troubled (perhaps even diagnosing the person, leading to a sense of being pathologized). Narrative therapists tend to develop **counter-documents**, which are documents that highlight the person's strengths and preferred identity. These may take the form of therapeutic letters, in which the therapist highlights how the client has begun to challenge the problem and take back their life. With younger clients, narrative therapists might give them certificates to mark their achievements. For instance, I was working with a 10-year-old boy who kept on getting into fights at school. We externalized fighting and talked about how fighting had gotten him into trouble at school and at home. We then discussed how, since he had now learned how to fight, he could fight fighting. Over the course of the next month, he did not have one fight. I then gave him the Fight Fighting Award (see Figure 9.8). Counter-documents can be photocopied and given to a wide variety

The Fight Fighting Award
This award is given to Mike Fernandez in recognition of his ability to fight Fighting. Fighting was dominating his life and getting him into trouble at school and home. Mike decided that he wasn't going to put up with Fighting's shenanigans anymore and used his fighting skills for his own good.
Michael D. Reiter
Michael D. Reiter, Ph.D., LMFT

Figure 9.8 A sample narrative certificate.

of people (what narrative therapists call "readship"), or placed on the refrigerator or wall to help remind the client of the positive changes they've made.

Termination occurs when clients have embraced their preferred ways of being, separating themselves from the oppression of the problem. This is a shift from the problem-saturated story that they held, based on allegiance to dominant discourses that were totalizing and limiting their identity, to an alternative story where they have more possibilities available and a preferred identity.

GLOSSARY

- **Complainant**: A person who perceives a problem but thinks someone else must change for things to get better.
- **Compliment**: Pointing out to the client actions they've taken to make their lives better.
- **Coping questions**: Questions designed to bring forth the actions of clients so their lives do not get worse than they currently are.
- **Counter-documents**: Written documents that highlight alternative stories of people that focus on their strengths and personal agency.
- **Customer**: A person who perceives a problem and thinks that their changing will improve the problem.
- **Definitional ceremony**: When people other than the clients and therapist observe the therapy session.
- **Dominant discourses**: Ideas and concepts that are prevalent within society and held as the social standard.
- **Exceptions**: Times when the problem could have happened but did not.

- **Externalizing**: Separating the person from the problem; talking about the problem as a living entity.
- **First session formula task**: Intervention given at the end of the first session that asks clients to pay attention the following week to what they want more of in their lives.
- **Landscape of action**: Parts of the client's story that focus on what occurred.
- **Landscape of identity**: Parts of the client's story that focus on how the client views themselves.
- **Miracle question**: Question designed to get clients to think about life without the problem and what they would be doing.
- **Outsider witness practices**: A group of people, usually past clients, who watch a session and provide feedback on what they were attuned to in the therapeutic talk while the client and therapist listen.
- **Postmodern therapies**: Models of therapy that operate from the premise that there is no absolute truth; rather, meaning is developed through conversation.
- **Presession change question**: Asking about what has been better since the client made the appointment.
- **Presupposition**: The expectation that something will happen.
- **Problem-saturated stories**: People's narratives that focus primarily on what is going wrong.
- **Problem talk**: Talk that focuses on what is going wrong.
- **Re-authoring**: Shifting the problem-saturated story to an alternative where the client has a different relationship to the problem and views themselves with more personal agency.
- **Reflecting team**: A group of therapists who watch a session and then provide feedback at some point during the session so that client and therapist can gain alternative perspectives.
- **Re-membering**: Conversations about how important people in the client's life view them and what they value in each other.
- **Scaling questions**: Questions that attempt to make an abstract concept concrete.
- **Skeleton keys**: Interventions that are useful for a wide array of people with a wide array of problems.
- **Solution-forced therapy**: Therapist position of only wanting to hear about good things rather than both problem and solution talk.
- **Solution talk**: Talk that focuses on what is going well.

- **Unique outcomes**: Times when the problem could have dominated the person, but the person did not allow this to happen.
- **What else questions**: Questions designed to introduce multiple pathways into a conversation.
- **Visitor**: A person who doesn't think they have a problem or want to do something about it.

CHAPTER SUMMARY

- SFBT focuses on past successful solutions and getting clients to do more of what has worked.
- Solution-focused therapists utilize a variety of questions (e.g., exception, scaling, and miracle) to help clients shift their lenses from problems to solutions.
- Solution-focused therapists help clients develop goals of what they want in their lives and connect them to past actions where they have been able to do so previously.
- Narrative therapy pays attention to how people and families internalize societal dominant discourses and then self-police and feel bad about themselves.
- Narrative therapists engage in scaffolding conversations where they help people to examine their relationship to the problem and bring forth the client's personal agency of how they have not let the problem oppress them.
- Narrative therapy highlights the alternative plotlines and local knowledge of people, shifting their experience from being a victim of the problem to being more heroic over the problem.

REFERENCES

Berg, I. K. (1994). *Family based services: A solution-focused approach.* Norton.

de Shazer, S. (1982). *Patterns of brief family therapy.* Guilford.

de Shazer, S. (1985). *Keys to solution in brief therapy.* Norton.

White, M. (2007). *Maps of narrative practice.* Norton.

White, M., & Epston, D. (1990). *Narrative means to therapeutic ends.* Norton.

DIVERSITY AND FAMILY THERAPY

Michael D. Reiter and Joshua L. Boe

ORIENTING QUESTIONS

- What is the impact of the client's and therapist's culture on what happens in the therapy room?
- How do family therapists utilize the notion of diversity in their practice?
- What role does social justice play for the family therapist?

Who are you? How would you describe yourself? How would you describe your family of origin? What are the components of self that you value most? What are the components that you use to identify yourself? What are the components that others use to identify you? How have these components changed over the years? How have they brought privilege into your life? What about discrimination and oppression? How are you similar to all other people? How are you unique? This chapter explores how family therapists explore these types of concepts for themselves and their clients, and how they have an impact in the therapy room, within a family, and between the family and society.

As discussed in Chapter 1, psychotherapy was born in Vienna, Austria. Freud, Jung, Adler, and Frankl started psychotherapy and its derivations, which then traveled to every corner of the world. From the early seeds of psychotherapy sown in the late 19th century, it has evolved to where we now have over 400 different models of therapy. As a class, family therapy developed in the late 1950s. Rather than being born in Europe, family therapy's primary history has deep

DOI: 10.4324/9781003312536-10

roots in the United States. Given this, the early models of therapy were developed by White Western cisgender heterosexual men, who worked primarily with White middle-class Western families.

Over time, family therapists began to recognize that the values they were using to understand family systems were based on White middle-class American families, and that those values might not be held or useful to the variety of families that therapists encounter. The early attempts to bring diversity into the family therapy zeitgeist focused primarily on the ethnicity of the family. Family therapist trainees were taught how Black families, Hispanic families, Asian families, and Native American families operated, and how this may be different from the standard North American family (White, middle-class, and Protestant).

The 1980s and early 1990s saw a surge in focus on multicultural counseling. Therapists attempted to understand how their clients were different from them. For the most part, therapists were White middle-class individuals working with clients who may or may not be. However, the field realized that not all therapists come from the majority culture. **Cross-cultural counseling** recognizes that there may be significant cultural differences between therapist and client (e.g., differences in race, gender, or ethnicity); but there are also other differences between people. For example, the therapist and client may both be White but come from quite different social classes, which can have a significant impact on their belief system, values, and behavior.

DIVERSITY

When family therapy first started, there was an exploration of diversity that was primarily based on race. Therapists explored what the differences might be between the standard North American family (White, middle class with two heterosexual parents) and non-White families, particularly Black and Hispanic. This then expanded to Asian, Middle Eastern, and other ethnic groups. These explorations were quite general, talking about these cultural groups as if everyone within them was similar. Luckily, the field began to examine the multitude of factors that comprise a family. You can do this exploration with your own family. What race would you say you come from? When family therapy first started, almost 70 years ago, this was a very easy question to answer: you were White, Black, Asian, etc. However, the current number of bi- and multi-racial individuals and families makes the conceptualization of a family based on a single factor, such as race, much more difficult. Even if you come from a primary racial group (e.g., both of your parents are White or both Black), you know that your family is not fully the same as other families with the same racial background. Other factors play a significant role in how your family experiences the world.

Family patterns are a combination of universal, culture-specific, and idiosyncratic ways of being. **Universally**, all families are tied together through relational bonds. These bonds and ways of being are culture specific, where, generally, some cultures have tighter bonds and others looser bonds. However, family patterns are also **idiosyncratic**, in that they are unique to that family. This understanding helped family therapists avoid having to start from scratch when they began working with a family. If the therapist is Bowenian, they understand that the family will engage in triangulation. The structural therapist knows the family will operate with some type of hierarchy. The MRI therapist knows the family will be engaging in failed solution attempts. Knowing something about the family's culture helps narrow the therapist's lens to how that family may tend to operate. But this doesn't mean the family will act in ways that reflect the stereotypical cultural rules and mores; they will have their own idiosyncratic ways of doing so.

Family therapy went on to explore issues of gender and the different expectations that society and families place on men and women. In the 1970s, there was a push in the field to explore gender dynamics not only in families, but in the field of family therapy, since the primary theories were developed by males who developed them within a patriarchal society. Family therapists began to incorporate ideas from **feminism**, which brought the notion of power dynamics into family therapists' perspectives and set the stage for the emergence of the postmodern family therapies that were to come.

Also, around the 1970s, in the United States and other Western countries, divorce became more common and accepted, and the organization of families began to change. Family therapists were increasingly working with single-parent and blended families. They needed to shift their understanding of traditional families and widen their lens to include a greater variety of families. So they needed to understand not only how families (and the people comprising them) might function differently from one another based on race and gender, but whether this was a first or second (or third or fourth) marriage and how stepfamilies operated differently than traditional intact families.

Around this time, immigration also increased, leading to White therapists encountering a greater variety of non-White families. Family therapists incorporated understandings of enculturation and acculturation to better understand the internal dynamics of the family, as well as the dynamics between the family and larger systems. **Enculturation** happens when you are raised within a culture and learn the rules and ways of that culture. **Acculturation** occurs when you enter a different culture and gradually learn its rules and ways. Family therapists needed to explore the immigration status of people, since acculturation usually places additional stressors on a family as their homeostasis needs to change to accommodate the new cultural context. Further, there are stressors that arise between recent immigrants and first-generation children. The young child may be the only person in the house to speak English and must act as a translator between the family and the outside world. Additionally, in all families, there is usually a generation gap that creates tension. In immigrant families, this gap is not only based on age, but on cultural ideas as the children are experiencing greater pressures of enculturation and acculturation. For instance, parents who were born and raised in Nicaragua will have different views of how families should be than their child who was born and raised in the United States and who is straddling Nicaraguan and US cultural expectations.

Family therapists then realized that cultural components are not universal. The experience of a Black female is different than that of a Black male. A Hispanic male single parent has different expectations placed on them and internal experiences than a married Hispanic male. A poor Asian individual experiences the world differently than a rich Asian individual. Thus, family therapists began to explore people's **intersectionality**: the points of connection between the variety of aspects of self that connect to the wider social world (see Figure 10.1). These include (but are not limited to) race, class, gender, sexuality, ability, age, religion, appearance, and education.

Intersectionality helps to delineate those aspects of a person's life in which they may experience privilege and oppression. Someone who is White receives many privileges in most parts of the world. A White uneducated person receives privilege from being White, but experiences aspects of oppression based on their social class. A Black female lesbian who is from a lower economic status is disadvantaged on multiple levels, as they are not in the majority group when it comes to race, class, gender, or sexual orientation. Any one of these aspects of oppression can be overwhelming for a person, let alone

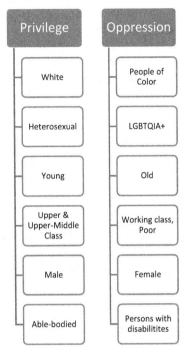

Figure 10.1 Intersectionality explores the overlapping and interlocking aspects of personhood that lead to privilege or oppression.

two or more marginalized aspects of personhood which are experienced at the same time.

Throughout the bulk of family therapy's history, most family therapists were White middle-class individuals. It is only recently that these therapists have become self-reflective to explore the White privilege that they benefit from in society as well as in the therapy room. **White privilege** encompasses the benefits that one receives from being White (and of the majority culture), which also disadvantages non-Whites. These benefits are often not seen but are systemically present. For instance, most actors on television are White; almost all politicians (and over 95% of all US Presidents) are White; and in most cities in the United States, Whites comprise a majority of the population. This representation in almost all facets of society affords certain benefits that non-Whites do not receive. While Whites have constituted the bulk of family therapy developers and practitioners, the landscape has been changing. Many more non-White therapists

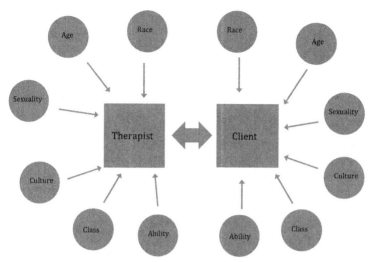

Figure 10.2 When therapists and clients interact, two (or more) people come together from two different social locations.

are now entering the field. This diversity can also be seen in other aspects, as the field is now dominated by females who are training to become family therapists.

We can also look at the intersectionality between therapist and client (see Figure 10.2). That is, each person comes from a certain **social location**, which is the position they hold in society based on all their characteristics. Previously, therapists may not have explored how the overlap between their social location and the client's social location impacted the therapeutic process (and recall from Chapter 4 where we discussed the importance of the therapeutic alliance). Today, this has become a key component of therapy, as therapists not only explore their privileges based on race, age, gender, etc., but also the privilege and power dynamics that come from being a therapist. Many try to reduce the power imbalance that occurs between therapist and client by not prescribing what the client must or should do, but by viewing themselves as a consultant to the client, who is really the expert on their own experience.

Multiculturalism is an appreciation of the cultural differences between people. All family therapy programs have at least one class that focuses on multiculturalism. The class may be titled differently but will focus on diversity—hopefully in its widest sense. However, the main accrediting body of family therapy graduate programs in the United States, the Commission on Accreditation for Marriage and Family Therapy Education, wants programs to ensure that aspects of diversity are explored in every single class! As we've been discussing, people are different in a wide range of areas. However, usually, for shorthand communication, we might call this "diversity" or "cultural differences."

Culture tends to be viewed primarily as ethnicity; however, its definition focuses on the ways and beings of a particular cultural group. These may be determined by age, race, education, nationality, etc. **Cross-cultural therapy** occurs when the therapist and client are from two different cultural groups (e.g., the therapist is Black and the client Native American; or the therapist is an immigrant from Israel while the client was born and raised in Missouri). Some clients prefer to have a therapist with a similar cultural background, thinking it will be easier for the therapist to understand them and the struggles they have gone through. While clients can decide to work or not work with a therapist based on one or more aspects of the therapist's culture (e.g., gender, sexual orientation, or race), therapists cannot. Family therapists must be open to working with any and all clients. This is part of our ethical codes and core competencies.

The notion of diversity is so important to family therapists that the American Association for Marriage and Family Therapy (AAMFT) has it as the first standard of responsibility to clients:

1.1 Non-Discrimination. Marriage and family therapists provide professional assistance to persons without discrimination on the basis of race, age, ethnicity, socioeconomic status, disability, gender, health status, religion, national origin, sexual orientation, gender identity or relationship status.

What this means is that family therapists work with all clients. However, they also must appreciate that the way they work may need to change based on the characteristics of clients. This is highlighted in the AAMFT Core Competencies.

4.3.2. Deliver interventions in a way that is sensitive to special needs of clients (e.g., gender, age, socioeconomic status, culture/race/ethnicity, sexual orientation, disability, personal history, larger systems issues of the client.

While we tend to focus on one aspect of a person's culture, individuals are inherently multicultural. We are impacted not only by one culture, but by many. When you think of yourself, explore your various social identities, including:

- age;
- race;
- ethnicity;
- gender;
- sex;
- sexual orientation;
- religion;
- social class;
- nation of origin; and
- citizenship.

Further, within each of these are subcultures. For instance, in the United States, there are differences based on location. Southerners, in some ways, are different from Northerners, who are different from Midwesterners. Southern Methodists are different from Southern atheists. Thus, we are always engaging in multicultural counseling, as all people are multicultural beings.

When you look at the above bullets, how do these aspects shape the way that you see the world? The way that others see you? Based on these components, what are your biases? How do they lead you to experience the world similar to other people? Different from other people? Family therapists try to explore their own biases to reduce their impact while they are in the therapy room. Further, they try to learn about the client's culture to ensure they are respecting who the client is and how the client understands the world.

From a Student's Perspective

As a young, first-generation Cuban cisgender heterosexual female currently studying family therapy, I've learned that every puzzle piece of an individual's identity is essential to understanding our biases, worldviews, and diversity. Through combining my work in domestic violence and the training I have received in my program thus far, I've realized that my identity influences not only how I view the world, but also how the world views me. One highlight piece of knowledge

I have acquired from my work with clients is the value of awareness when it comes to our socioeconomic status and the limitations/opportunities that result from it. Uniting my clients' backgrounds and my firsthand position as part of an underserved community has allowed me to appreciate the resilience that comes from blending differences and similarities in the therapy room. Putting this understanding into practice has widened my capacity to apply the concept of unique experiences as individuals in relationships develop a broader, empathetic, and culturally aware lens when approaching my clients.

Nailin Morera, master's student

SOCIAL JUSTICE

One of the recent explorations in family therapy is a focus on **social justice**, which is how power differentials entitle one group to benefits at the expense of another. These benefits or advantages are experienced within different contexts (i.e., individual, community, and wider society) across our lives. In the individual context, power differentials often go unnoticed, especially for those who benefit from them. Here is an example of the individual context. Consider for a moment a police officer pulls you over. Depending on your skin color, the extent of your worries differs. If you are a White person, you are not likely to be too terrified of being pulled over. At worst, you may feel anxious, frustrated, or annoyed about the encounter. The thought of death during a traffic stop rarely crosses White people's minds, as it does for people of color—especially given the current social context. In this example, White people aren't acting any different than people of color; but because of White privilege, the experience varies greatly. Power and privilege also occur at the community level. For example, if you are in a wealthier county, you tend to have greater access to resources compared to those in poorer counties. This inequitable distribution of resources can negatively impact those in poorer counties. Lastly, at the societal level, we can see the influence of power and privilege in state and federal legislation that is introduced and at times passed. Often, privileged groups are not directly impacted by legislation that is aimed at the oppressed group. For example, cisgender men are not impacted by access to reproduction rights or bodily autonomy in the same way that cisgender women and transgender people are. Such issues are currently impacting our and our clients' lives. Given the systemic nature of these power differentials, family therapists leverage social justice to disrupt these inequities.

Incorporating social justice into therapy can initially be daunting. Questions of how best to do so creep in, making us feel like it must be through large gestures and direct conversations that name all the systems that we outlined above. We will offer a few ways that therapists can incorporate these ideas into their practice with clients. First, socially just-oriented therapists question the myth of neutrality. This myth refers to the assumption that therapists are trained to be neutral in the therapy room and to only discuss what the client wants to discuss. Conversely, socially just-oriented therapists acknowledge that remaining neutral in the room often serves to reinforce systems of power and privilege. Second, case conceptualization through a social justice lens entails examining the wider societal context and the influence of power, privilege, and oppression. Consider a heterosexual couple, comprised of a cisgender man and a cisgender woman, who present to therapy with communication issues (a very common complaint). A therapist who is not guided by social justice may simply work with the couple on resolving the complaint without considering how gender dynamics may be contributing to the complaint. A socially just-oriented therapist considers how gender power dynamics may shape relational issues. They may explore with the couple how they were taught to be in relationships and how gender influences those roles. They may explore how the couple makes decisions. Such explorations allow the couple to take a different position in their relationship if they desire.

Third, socially just-oriented therapists consider power, privilege, and oppression in their delivery of services. When working with low-income families, we need to ensure our interventions are responsive. We cannot expect any of our clients, regardless of social class, to pay for extra materials to engage in the interventions that we think will be beneficial. For example, is a sticker chart the only way to track a child's behavioral change and reinforce positive behaviors? Is a self-help book that important for a client's understanding of an idea we present to them? Being responsive requires that we be creative in our interventions and think outside the theories that were developed with certain demographics in mind. Lastly, developing critical consciousness can impact therapists' and clients' lives. Critical consciousness brings awareness of the sociopolitical context of daily life, which impacts both therapists and clients. For therapists, developing this awareness allows us to avoid replicating power and privilege in our interventions. For clients, it enables them to gain a meta-perspective of the distress they are experiencing (Almeida et al., 2008). For example, depression and anxiety may be more than a "chemical imbalance" and a symptom of oppression a client is experiencing. Socially just-oriented therapists may utilize consciousness-raising activities to develop critical consciousness.

FROM CULTURAL COMPETENCE TO CULTURAL RESPONSIVENESS

As we outlined earlier, the field of family therapy has evolved. In line with this evolution, the field has made important strides in addressing cultural sensitivity and multiculturalism. Terms such as "culturally competent," "cultural sensitivity," "cultural humility," and "culturally responsive" are often used interchangeably. However, there are important differences between these terms. When therapists say they are **culturally competent**, they are saying that they hold expert knowledge because they have learned about a minoritized group. Because they hold this expert knowledge, they then hold expertise over what that minoritized group needs, without first checking in with the local community. When therapists say they are **culturally responsive**, they are relying on that community's local knowledge about what is needed. In addition, they are held accountable to that local community. By providing these definitions, we are not suggesting that therapists need not educate themselves about other cultures. We want to situate that holding knowledge does not make us an expert on the needs of "others." When therapists take the stance of expert, they often unintentionally perpetuate power, privilege, and oppression. By taking a stance of responsiveness, therapists can be more mindful of the power they hold and how they use this power, regardless of how much we know it is imperative for us to remain curious and honor our clients' lived experiences.

LGBTQIA CLIENTS

Before we conclude this chapter, we want to provide you with some information that may be helpful when working with LGBTQIA clients. This is limited to a brief introduction, and it would be irresponsible to suggest that this is *all* you need to know. Like those of other cultural groups, the experiences of LGBTQIA people are complex and connected to the other social locations we presented earlier. In addition, our understanding and language used within this population continue to shift. One example of how language has changed is the usage of "queer" and "homosexual." "Homosexual" used to be the term used to define sexual minorities; however, it is outdated and rooted in pathology. Interestingly, "queer" has historically been used as a slur for the LGBTQIA population, but in recent decades the community has been reclaiming "queer" and using it as an identifier. As society's understanding of the community has changed, therapists have had to adjust their work with LGBTQIA clients.

Although the field has made progress in providing inclusive and affirming LGBTQIA services, we cannot overlook how psychotherapists have marginalized LGBTQIA identities. "Homosexuality" was considered a mental health diagnosis in the *Diagnostic and Statistical Manual of Mental Disorders* (*DSM*) prior to being removed in 1973. This removal marked an important shift in de-pathologizing sexual identities. With respect to gender identities, "transsexualism" was replaced with "gender identity disorder" in the fourth edition of the *DSM*. Gender identity disorder was later removed from the fifth edition of the *DSM*; however, gender dysphoria remains a diagnosis. Although the intention was to de-pathologize transgender and nonbinary gender identities, gender dysphoria still conflates social identity with a mental disorder. In fact, psychotherapists were often given the role of gatekeeper for transgender and nonbinary clients wanting to undergo medical transitions. Beyond the *DSM*, there is a current ethical debate on whether it is ethical to refer out an LGBTQIA client because of the therapist's beliefs (Hecker & Murphy, 2015). There are some who would posit it is unethical for us to refer out because of our beliefs. These therapists often cite this as a violation of the non-discrimination clause as outlined by the AAMFT's ethical codes. Conversely, there are those who suggest that if it would cause harm to the client, it would be best for the therapist to refer them out. However, this stance does not require that therapists engage in self-of-therapist work to address their biases. What is interesting about this "ethical dilemma" is that we rarely see it playing out with other social identities. Lastly, there are current therapeutic practices directed at changing minoritized sexual and gender identities. Such practices have been called "reparative therapy", "reorientation therapy," "sexual identity change efforts," and "gender identity change efforts." The goal of these practices is to assist clients in living out a heterosexual or cisgender identity. Many states have banned such services for youth as they cause further harm; nor does research support their utility. As alluded to previously, family therapists have long challenged the pathologizing of LGBTQIA people.

In 2022, the AAMFT put forward clinical guidelines for LGBTQIA affirming marriage and family therapy. These guidelines rest upon five pillars: intersectional, systemic, relational, liberatory, and transformative (see Figure 10.3). The **intersectional pillar** holds, as we have previously explained, that people live at the intersection of many overlapping and interlocking systems, including identity, power, privilege, and oppression. The **systemic pillar** highlights the notion—which you've hopefully gleaned from this book—that individuals do not operate in isolation. They always behave within contexts, particularly relationships and cultural power structures. The **relational pillar** holds that people influence and are influenced by their connections to other individuals, families, groups, and communities. The **liberatory pillar** establishes the notion that family therapists must separate and liberate themselves from the systems of oppression that have existed within societies. This is where self-of-the-therapist work is extremely important. The **transformative pillar** empowers family therapists not only to challenge their own beliefs and practices that are based on supremacism, but to transform the larger systems that they (and thus clients) encounter. Thus, this pillar is about making systemic change beyond the family.

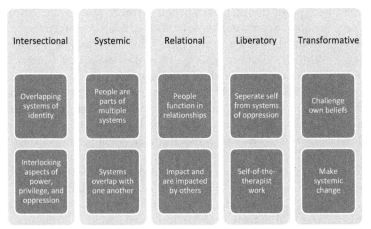

Figure 10.3 The AAMFT has put forth guidelines for clinical practice with LBGTQIA clients that rest upon five pillars.

GLOSSARY

- **Acculturation**: How people develop values, beliefs, and behaviors when they assimilate to a different culture than they were born and raised in.
- **Cross-cultural therapy**: Therapy between two people who have significant cultural differences, such as race, gender, or ethnicity.
- **Culturally responsive**: Being attuned to a community's local knowledge rather than entering with an expert knowledge position.
- **Culture**: The beliefs, rituals, and social organization of a group of people.
- **Diversity**: The acknowledgment that people have different social and ethnic backgrounds and come from different genders and sexual orientations.
- **Enculturation**: How people develop values, beliefs, and behaviors when born and raised in a culture.
- **Feminism**: Originally focusing on women's rights, feminism promotes the reduction of power imbalances between people.
- **Idiosyncrasy**: Ways of being and thinking that are unique to a person or family.
- **Intersectionality**: Focuses on how people and/or groups have overlapping systems of discrimination and privilege.
- **Multicultural**: When people of two or more different cultures interact.
- **Social justice**: A movement toward an equitable distribution of opportunities in society.
- **Social location**: The various factors that a person is situated in, including their race, social class, sexual orientation, geographic location, gender, age, and ability.
- **Universality**: Processes that are consistent across all people and all social groups.
- **White privilege**: The advantages that White people have by being part of the majority in a culture.

CHAPTER SUMMARY

- Family therapy was initially developed primarily by White Western males based on a patriarchal society.
- Family therapists have attempted to explore diversity aspects, which include therapist, client, and larger social systems.

- Family therapists explore people's intersectionality and how issues of privilege and oppression impact individuals.
- Culturally responsive therapy prompts the therapist to work with clients in a way that is responsive to the local community's knowledge. This shifts the expertise from the therapist to the client.
- The notion of diversity in therapy has been continuously changing, leading therapists to have a better appreciation of the unique contexts and struggles of clients from a multitude of backgrounds and situations.

REFERENCES

Almeida, R. V., Dolan-Del Vecchio, K., & Parker, L. (2008). *Transformative family therapy: Just families in a just society*. Pearson.

Hartwell, E. E., Belous, C. K., et al. (2021). *Clinical guidelines for LGBTQIA affirming marriage and family therapy*. AAMFT.

Hecker, L., & Murphy, M. J. (2015). Contemporary and emerging ethical issues in family therapy. *Australian & New Zealand Journal of Family Therapy, 36*(4), 467–479. https://doi.org/10.1002/anzf.1121

McDowell, T., Knudson-Martin, C., & Bermudez, J. M. (2018). *Socioculturally attuned family therapy*. Routledge.

THE FUTURE OF FAMILY THERAPY

Michael D. Reiter and John K. Miller

ORIENTING QUESTIONS

- How is the field of family therapy continuing to grow and move into non-traditional work settings?
- How is family therapy useful in only a single session?
- What are some of the implications of family therapy expanding internationally?

Congratulations! You've made it to the end of the book. I know this has been a very quick journey through the world of family therapy, but we've covered a lot of ground and many years. We started, in Chapter 1, about 70 years ago, exploring how family therapy started. We then discussed how therapy is based on a code of ethics, which sets out the guidelines on how therapists should interact with clients. We've covered the systemic foundation of the field, the core skills, and the primary theoretical models of family therapy. We just discussed how family therapists understand the notion of diversity and how it impacts their practice. In this last chapter, we look ahead, outlining where we are now and where we are likely to go in the future. This may be the most important chapter for you, as hopefully, after reading this book, you've been inspired to become a family therapist. If so, then *you* will be the future of the field.

EXPANSION OF WORK ENVIRONMENTS

When you think about being a family therapist, how do you envision your day will go? Probably, you see yourself driving to a nice building

DOI: 10.4324/9781003312536-11

in a nice neighborhood where you enter a nice office. You've decorated it with warm tones and inviting furniture. Throughout the day, you work with five to eight families, and you make a lot of money! Most people, when going into the therapy field, envision working in private practice. This will give you the most freedom, as you can set your own hours and are beholden only to yourself. Further, if you dislike your boss, you only have yourself to blame (or to complain to).

While private practice is the primary work environment for family therapists, there are a variety of other ways that you can use your skills to help others. This section highlights a few of these possible pathways. As explained in Chapter 1, before you can work on your own, you must complete education and supervised clinical hours to become licensed. Many therapists, once they graduate, have about two years of full-time clinical work to complete to become licensed. They tend to do this in an agency setting. This might involve working in a substance abuse facility, a residential setting, or a school; or on other programs that provide services for individuals, couples, families, or groups.

What else might you be able to do with your degree and your knowledge? You can choose the path that we've chosen, which is teaching. To become a teacher of family therapy, you will need to get your doctoral degree. Most family therapy programs will give you a Ph.D. in family therapy, while others have what is called a DMFT. The Ph.D. is a bit more research oriented, while the DMFT is more clinical. Either way, you will be eligible to become a faculty member at a university and train the next generation of family therapists.

If you choose a clinical pathway, you can do therapy in your own office, an agency, a religious setting, a Native American reservation, a hospital, a university student counseling center, or the corporate field. Michael's best friend earned his Ph.D. in family therapy and became a licensed marriage and family therapist. However, he didn't want to go into private practice or engage in traditional therapy, as he also enjoyed business systems. So he became an organizational consultant and is now the director of training and development for a very large medical organization. He gets to fly around the country working with doctors, nurses, and other healthcare professionals, troubleshooting whenever they have interpersonal issues within their departments. He uses everything he has learned about how systems operate and change to help the functioning of his company.

One of the newest areas that family therapists have ventured into is coaching. This is not the athletic coaching that you may have experienced in your youth. Rather, it involves coaching people to develop and achieve clear and specific goals. While the two fields are not the same, there is a lot of overlap between the two. Probably the biggest difference is the temporal focus: therapy tends to be present and past oriented, while coaching is more present and future oriented. Coaching is more behavioral, not focusing on the more emotional or meaning aspects of personhood, but rather helping people figure out how to develop pathways to clear and measurable goals.

From a Student's Perspective

As a marriage and family therapy student, I was taught to understand my clients' problems and challenges systemically. I was also taught that clients are the experts in their own lives and have the tools and resources needed to be well. Now, as a psychedelic integration therapist (where clients ingest legal psychedelics overseen by a medical professional and then receive therapeutic services), I have found that clients can arrive at that systemic understanding rather quickly and on their own through a psychedelic session. In that session, they often experience that absolutely all is connected and relational, as well as tapping into their inner intelligence. That experience and insight can bring about the change needed—perceptually and behaviorally—to create a positive difference in my clients' lives.

Vanessa Bibliowicz, doctoral student

TELEHEALTH

In March 2020, the world experienced something that we had not known for over 100 years. The coronavirus pandemic confused, scared, and overwhelmed us. It led to most countries instituting lockdowns, when people only went out of their houses for the bare necessities of food or medicine. Many businesses shut down and millions upon millions of people who were receiving medical and mental health services went without. Michael was working in a university family therapy clinic where one day we were seeing clients and the next day the doors were shut. There were clients who needed services and student therapists who now had no clients.

Luckily, all was not lost. For some years prior, therapists had been dipping their toes into the world of **telehealth**—the provision of healthcare services via technology. Since the advent of the internet over 50 years ago, therapists had been experimenting with using email in therapy. As technology became more advanced, the possibility of teleconferencing emerged. Therapists had been quite hesitant to incorporate this medium into mainstream practice because it presented some potential problems, such as how to guarantee confidentiality for the client, and how to ensure that you are following the appropriate laws and rules (given that either you, the client, or both could be anywhere in the world when meeting via video), as well as ensuring the client's safety (e.g., what to do if you think the client is homicidal or suicidal).

When the lockdowns happened, therapists scrambled, knowing there were millions of people who needed their services. Telehealth was the answer. Regulatory bodies relaxed their guidelines on who could use videoconferencing and how they could do so. Thousands upon thousands of therapists who had never conducted a video session, or even thought about doing so, were suddenly at home on their computers talking with clients who were on their own computers at home. Therapists got a peek into clients' domestic lifestyles and clients got a more personalized view of their therapists. For instance, Michael's clients got to see his cat Piper, who likes to sit right next to him when he is on video so she can be petted.

Therapists also discovered that their commute was cut out. No longer did we need to walk, bike, drive, bus, or train to work. We didn't have to wake up so early or come home so late. We could dress a little less formally and potentially could save a lot of money by not having to rent an office. Further, it cut down the number of cancellations and no-shows by clients. Previously, a client might cancel a session if they couldn't find childcare or were sick. Now, these events no longer prevent them from attending the session. They can wake up, stay in bed, open their laptop or the link they receive from the therapist on their smartphone, and have their session. This seems like a win–win situation for both therapist and client. For family therapists, this also adds the potential of having more family members attend a session, as children, parents, and grandparents who live in different cities can all log on at the same time to participate.

Before the pandemic, few therapists were interested in telehealth, as they thought that remote therapy would lose the intimacy factor. Since the pandemic, however, most therapists have engaged in telehealth and will likely utilize it to some degree in their practice. Telehealth is here to stay and will only grow in popularity and frequency.

EMPIRICALLY VALIDATED TREATMENT

When family therapy was being developed, successful therapy was measured by the therapist's perception of the session. They used their observations to see if the family changed in ways they thought would be useful for them. Clients were then asked about the usefulness of therapy and their self-reports were taken as success. However, over the last 20 to 30 years, insurance companies and managed care agencies are holding therapists more accountable for positive change.

Previously, therapists could use any modality they wanted with clients, basing the decision on their training and preference. However, managed care agencies began relying upon scientific evidence in a bid to ensure therapists were engaging in best practices. The outcome of this was a push for **empirically validated treatment approaches**: therapies that have been scientifically tested to prove their effectiveness. This push is also known as **evidence-based practice**.

To help us understand this concept better, let's switch to something that you do (hopefully) every week. How do you know which is the best laundry detergent? Do you take it on faith when a company tells you its product is good at cleaning clothes? Do you go with the cheapest? I'm sure you've watched countless television advertisements that compare two products and show you how one paper towel, dog food, or laundry detergent is better than another. How do they know that it is? They've done (hopefully, if they are being honest and operating from a place of integrity) research studies.

Empirically validated treatment approaches are those models of therapy that have been utilized in research studies and have proved to be effective. While many different research designs can be used, there are two that are most commonly used in this area. The first involves getting a group of people (called a **sample**) and randomly giving half of them therapy and the other half no therapy. The first half (who get therapy) is called the **experimental group**, while the second half (who don't get therapy; they are usually kept on a waiting list for therapy) is called the **control group**. Given that individuals have been randomly assigned to one of these two groups, they should initially be the same on any measure you give them. After some time (perhaps two months, but it can be any amount of time), one group has had therapy and the other has not. The two groups are then given the same measurement (probably regarding the degree of distress they are experiencing) to see if there is a difference (see Figure 11.1). The

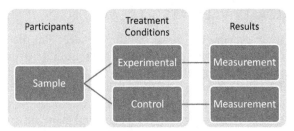

Figure 11.1 In a simple between-subjects design experiment, the sample is randomly assigned to one of two conditions and then given the same assessment to see if one treatment condition impact scores on the measurement.

idea is that the experimental group will have higher positive scores (e.g., happiness or good relationships) and lower negative scores (e.g., depression or conflict). If so, that model can be said to be empirically validated (although one study is not definitive—many studies need to be conducted to ensure there wasn't a fluke in the research).

You might be saying to yourself, "Of course the experimental group did better. They got therapy and the other group did not." Good. This is what you should be saying. To deal with this, researchers also conduct comparison studies. In these studies, a group of participants will be randomly assigned to one of two (or more) treatment modalities. Perhaps one group gets four months of Bowenian therapy, and the other group gets four months of structural therapy. At the end of the study, everyone is given the same measurement tool (e.g., an assessment that measures a family's level of cohesion). Both groups have received therapy, so if there is a difference in the group averages on the assessment, it shouldn't be because one group had therapy and the other didn't; rather, it should be based on the type of therapy.

What we've found so far—which is very good news for therapists— is that therapy is better for people than no therapy! We've also found that one model of therapy isn't necessarily better than another. However, what more and more researchers are exploring now is whether a certain model is better for a certain type of client with a certain type of problem. For example, is solution-focused therapy better for adolescents who are dealing with substance abuse issues? Or is narrative therapy better for anorexic clients than Freudian psychoanalysis? The future of family therapy will likely see an increase in therapists engaging in research—or at least reading the research—to explore which approaches have been shown to be effective.

SINGLE-SESSION THERAPY

So far, we have discovered that all models of therapy have proven to be effective. This is great news! However, there is another dilemma in the world of therapy: the problem of clinical service delivery. This concerns how people receive services from a provider. For instance, if there is a medication that can treat a certain illness with very good results, we may still have the problem of getting that medication to the people who need it when they need it. In the world of therapy, it turns out we have very good methods to treat most problems; but one dilemma is that many of the people who would benefit from treatment don't seek help. We know from our studies that about half of the people in the USA at some time in their life would benefit from seeing a therapist, yet fewer than half of those people actually do so. The three main reasons for this are that people feel ashamed to ask for help (stigma); they believe it will be too expensive; or they don't know which therapist to go to.

Single-session therapy (SST) is a type of clinical service delivery designed to overcome people's resistance to seeking out help. Since the dawn of therapy, we have worked on the assumption that change is difficult; that people are often resistant; and that it takes time to help. People that came to treatment only once and didn't return were considered treatment failures and it was assumed that they had received no benefit from their single session. Yet it turns out this assumption was incorrect. In the early 1990s, a few pioneering researchers began to study those people that only came once and discovered that the majority were not actually treatment failures, but had benefited enough from their single session that they did not feel the need to return. Further studies showed that for many of these people, the changes were not temporary, but lasting. These findings gave birth to the field of SST. One of the main features of SST was to organize the treatment to provide the greatest help possible in a single meeting with a therapist. The therapist providing the service may use many different therapy models, but generally holds onto the idea that they should do the best they can with the client in their meeting. Various SST centers were developed across North America in the late 1990s and studies were conducted on those services. They showed that SST did a good job of overcoming the barriers to service. People that would not consider going to traditional therapy were much more likely to avail of SST. Another finding was that SST attracted one group that is typically more resistant to going to therapy: men. In a typical traditional therapy service, only 20% of the people that go are men. Yet in SST services, about 50% of the people that go are men. We also learned that SST attracted people that are resistant to going to regular therapy; yet after their SST session, they reported they were much more likely to seek out longer-term therapy in the future if they had the need. For most of these people, SST was their first therapy experience. As we have seen outside restaurants in shopping mall food courts, it can be helpful to give out a small sample of the good things that are provided inside to attract people to come in and enjoy a full meal. In the following decades, hundreds of SST services have been developed in North America and around the world in hospitals, community agencies, universities, emergency services (e.g., Red Cross), and social services agencies.

So, what exactly happens in an SST session? Well, the therapist providing the service is usually also a regular traditional therapist, with all the skills and techniques needed for that job. They embrace a few assumptions and practices that help make the most out of a single therapeutic opportunity. These basic assumptions include the following:

- It is possible for people to benefit from a single therapeutic meeting: This is important because if the therapist does not believe this, it will be communicated to the client and it is unlikely any meaningful change will actually occur.
- Time is important: The SST therapist focuses on making the most out of the time they have. A typical session is only one hour. This means they must attend to what the client needs now and in the future, rather than focusing on the past. Other forms of therapy dive into detailed and exhaustive explorations of the past; but in SST, the focus tends to be on the present and the future.
- "More is not better"; "better is better": This is a way of saying that providing more treatment and intervention is not always better; and that the therapist should provide the right amount of intervention and treatment to assist the particular client they are working with.
- There should be some outcome at the end of the meeting: This may be a suggestion to try something in the session, or something they take home and try. It may be some advice or information about the problem. The intervention may involve a reframing (creating another story) of the situation

they are dealing with. It may also be a recommendation to seek out further assistance from another service (e.g., traditional therapy, medical treatment, psychiatric services, social services agencies).

- The "ripple effect": The object of the SST meeting is not to solve all problems of the client, but simply to get them started in the right direction. This is commonly known as the "ripple effect" in therapy. The idea is that the SST is a starting point and is like a small pebble thrown into a lake: the ripples spread out across the lake in time and can potentially have a dramatic effect.

- People are fundamentally healthy and resourceful: SST therapists believe that people are fundamentally healthy and resourceful, rather than sick and weak. From this point of view, the therapist is always trying to find ways to recognize and enhance the strengths the client already possesses. This may also include considering resources like family, friends, and community.

- Timing is important: It is imperative in an SST service to see the client as soon as possible once they decide to seek help. People are most likely to change when they are immediately dealing with the problem. As the old saying goes, "Strike while the iron is hot."

In the SST session, the therapist tries to make the most of their time with the client by streamlining the paperwork and intake procedure. In some services, clients don't even need to make an appointment, but can be seen on a walk-in basis. For instance, if a young person gets in trouble at school, which is likely to cause conflict in the family, the entire family could be seen by the therapist the same day and a potential crisis could be averted.

In the session, the therapist typically asks questions that focus on the current situation and directs the client to think about what they need in the future. These questions might include the following:

- "How would you describe the problem today and what would you like to get out of the session?"
- "How would we know that this session had been useful to you?"
- "What have you tried in the past that helped?"
- "What are some things you haven't yet tried, but that you think might help?"

- "If the problem disappeared tomorrow, what other problems might you have?"
- "What is one small step we might take today that would be a step in the right direction?"

The SST therapist usually provides the client with feedback and suggestions in the following areas at the end of the session:

- compliments, commendations, and validations;
- follow-up questions about the situation, to gain clarity and stimulate positive solutions;
- alternative stories (reframes) that could be used to describe the situation in a different way; and
- interventions, either in the session or as homework.

Major Players

Dr. Moshe Talmon (1950–) was born on a kibbutz in Israel and eventually earned his Ph.D. in clinical psychology from the University of Pennsylvania in 1982. He then interned at the Philadelphia Child Guidance Clinic under the supervision of Salvador Minuchin. He was one of the first researchers to explore the potential of SST. He studied the records of thousands of people that came to therapy only once and discovered that many had not failed in treatment, but had benefited greatly from a single session. He is currently a senior lecturer at Tel Aviv University and at the Academic College of Tel Aviv-Yaffo in Israel. Talmon is also the founder and director of the International Center for SST. Some of his most influential books include *Single-Session Therapy: Maximizing the Effect of the First (and Often Only) Therapeutic Encounter* and *Single Session Solutions: A Guide to Practical, Effective and Affordable Therapy*.

INTERNATIONAL FAMILY THERAPY

Although family therapy was largely developed in the West, since the turn of the century it has spread all over the world. While most family therapy techniques and theories were developed in the US, the country is home to only about 5% of the world's population, with the majority of the people on the planet living in Asia (85%).

Many non-US countries were interested in learning about the new techniques and methods of family therapy. In the early 2000s, family therapy began to spread throughout the world through educational exchanges between faculty, scholars, and students from various countries. US scholars were invited to teach about family therapy on almost every continent, while also learning about indigenous ways of treating and healing people with therapy needs. The US hosted an ever-increasing number of international students for university study. While family therapy was somewhat new on the planet, almost every culture in the world has some forms of "therapeutic" treatment practices that are valuable for everyone to learn. For instance, in Central and South America, it has been historically common for people to seek out the help of a shaman (a community holy person) for advice and intervention in difficult times. The indigenous people of Australia also have a cultural tradition of shamans that advise people when they need help. In Asia, it has been historically common for people to seek out the help of "fortune tellers/advice givers," who can usually be found outside the walls of Buddhist monasteries and will talk with people about their problems and suggest solutions for a small donation. In Cambodia and throughout Southeast Asia, people often see a "traditional healer" when in need. While the Western world was eager to share the methods of family therapy they had developed, they had to be cautious to avoid imposing their values and culture on others without considering the potential negative consequences. Many Asian cultures have historically suffered under previous "colonial" expansions into their countries from Western powers, often with disastrous consequences for those being colonized.

With a desire to avoid these negative "colonialist" traditions of the past, many of the Western therapists that engaged in international therapy and teaching were careful to avoid being oppressive or overbearing in these exchanges. Three common principles guided these pioneering therapists to avoid the unintended consequences of introducing new ideas from outside:

- Universalism: This involves considering which elements, for what is being discussed, are universal and shared by all human beings on the planet. Which elements of intervention are universal to human beings in general?
- Essentialism (indigenization): This involves recognizing which elements of the culture are essential to the culture being addressed.

These include elements that are so unique and individual to the culture being dealt with that they cannot be changed much without negative effects on the culture or tradition.

- Imperialism: Which elements of intervention would be destructive, in an imperialistic way, if introduced to a new culture?

The methods of family therapy should thus be modified and shaped to fit the culture they are dealing with. For instance, in Southeast Asia, it is often difficult or impossible to have people in need come to meet a therapist in their office. Most people live in rural villages in farming communities spread out throughout the country. With this in mind, the early generations of family therapists in Cambodia created "mobile mental health units" that involved driving to rural villages and offering sessions with individuals and families on the go—often out in an open area in the village or in the farmland. Other times, the mobile mental health unit would go to people's houses at the invitation of families who requested help. This represents an important aspect of the need to adapt Western methods of family therapy to non-Western cultures. The last few decades have seen a rapid increase in the development of family therapy all over the world. The next generation of family therapists have an exciting and important role to play on the world stage.

Dr. John K. Miller and Dr. Xiaoi Fang organized one of the first generations of family therapy doctoral students in Beijing in the early 2000s. Through a generous Fulbright grant from the US Department of State and the Council for the International Exchange of Scholars, this collaborative group conducted a year-long family therapy teaching, research, and clinical service in China. The program continues to this day.

In the early 2000s, Dr. John K. Miller and Dr. Jason J. Platt began conducting international exchanges between family therapy students in Cambodia and the US. The exchange trips have occurred every year and have resulted in hundreds of students learning about both the practice of family therapy in the West and the emerging practices of family therapy in Southeast Asia.

The future of family therapy is definitely an international endeavor. There will be a mutual exchange of ideas, merging Western and Eastern ideas of personhood and change. This process will require mutual understanding and respect, allowing for a proliferation of therapeutic ideas and continued growth in our field.

GLOSSARY

- **Control condition**: A group of participants who are similar to the experimental group but do not get the intervention.
- **Empirically validated treatment approaches**: Models of therapy that have been shown, through research studies, to be effective.
- **Essentialism**: Aspects of a culture that are so integral to it that changing them will negatively impact the culture and its traditions.
- **Experimental condition**: A group of participants in a research study who receive the intervention (in therapy studies, they receive a form of therapy).
- **Imperialism**: Extending a country's influence through democracy or force.
- **Sample**: A group of people who participate in a study.
- **Single-session therapy**: Clinical service that is designed to be a one-time meeting between therapist and client.
- **Telehealth**: The use of technology (primarily videoconferencing) to engage in therapeutic services.
- **Universalism**: Aspects of personhood that are shared by all people, regardless of race, age, gender, or geography.

CHAPTER SUMMARY

- Family therapists primarily work in private practice settings.
- Family therapists also work in agencies, residential settings, hospitals, schools, and business organizations.
- Over the last few years, most family therapists have begun meeting clients both in person and online via telehealth (videoconferencing).
- Family therapy is attempting to research the various models to demonstrate that they are an empirically validated treatment method, thus showing their effectiveness.
- In empirically validated treatment studies, clients are randomly assigned to receive therapy or remain on a waiting list (or receive a different type of therapy) to determine which condition is more effective.
- SST attempts to help clients, in one session, to move forward in their lives, focusing on outcomes.

- SST is predicated on the notion that people can quickly change.
- International family therapy appreciates that Western ideas and practices may not be in line with non-Western cultures.
- International family therapy attempts to promote both universal and essential aspects of personhood based on the culture in which one is practicing.

REFERENCES

Talmon, M. (1991). *Single session therapy: Maximizing the effect of the first (and often only) therapeutic encounter.* Jossey-Bass.

Talmon, M. (1993). *Single-session solutions: A guide to practical, effective, and affordable therapy.* Da Capo Lifelong Books.

BIBLIOGRAPHY

Almeida, R. V., Dolan-Del Vecchio, K., & Parker, L. (2008). *Transformative family therapy: Just families in a just society*. Pearson.

Anderson, H. (1997). *Conversation, language, and possibilities*. Basic Books.

Aponte, H. J., & Kissil, K. (2016). *The person of the therapist training model*. Routledge.

Bateson, G. (1972). *Steps to an ecology of mind*. Ballantine.

Bateson, G., Jackson, D. D., Haley, J., & Weakland, J. (1956). Toward a theory of schizophrenia. *Behavioral Sciences, 1*, 251–264.

Becvar, D. S., & Becvar, R. J. (1999). *Systems theory and family therapy* (2nd ed.). University Press of America.

Berg, I. K. (1994). *Family based services: A solution-focused approach*. Norton.

Berg, I. K., & de Shazer, S. (1993). Making numbers talk: Language in therapy. In S. Friedman (Ed.). *The new language of change* (pp. 5–24). Guilford.

Boscolo, L., & Bertrando, P. (1993). *The times of time*. Norton.

Boscolo, L., Cecchin, G., Hoffman, L., & Penn, P. (1987). *Milan systemic family therapy*. Basic Books.

Boston, P. (2007). Therapeutic groundhog day—exploring the impact of the theory/approach on the self of the therapist. *Journal of Family Therapy, 29*, 338–341.

Boszormenyi-Nagy, I. (1987). *Foundations of contextual therapy*. Brunner/Mazel.

Boszormenyi-Nagy, I., Grunebaum, J., & Ulrich, D. (1991). Contextual therapy. In A. S. Gurman, & D. P. Kniskern (Eds.). *Handbook of family therapy: Volume II* (pp. 200–238). Brunner/Mazel.

Boszormenyi-Nagy, I., & Krasner, B. R. (1986). *Between give and take*. Brunner/Mazel.

Boszormenyi-Nagy, I., & Spark, G. (1984). *Invisible loyalties*. Brunner/Mazel.

Bowen, M. (1992). *Family therapy in clinical practice*. Jason Aronson.

Boyd-Franklin, N. (2003). *Black families in therapy* (2nd ed.). Guilford.

Bronfenbrenner, U. & Morris, P. A. (2006). The bioecological model of human development. In W. Damon & R. M. Lerner (Eds.). *Handbook of child psychology* (pp. 993–1023). John Wiley & Sons.

Carlson, T. S., Erickson, M. J., McGeorge, C. R., & Bermudez, J. M. (2004). *Just therapy with Latino families in the Midwestern United States*. Poster session presented at the Narrative Therapy and Community Work Conference, Oaxaca, Mexico.

Cecchin, G. (1987). Hypothesizing, circularity, and neutrality revisited: An invitation to curiosity. *Family Process, 26* (4), 405–413.

Cecchin, G., Lane, G., & Ray, W. (1993). *Irreverence: A strategy for therapists' survival*. Routledge.

Charlés, L. L. (2020). *International family therapy*. Routledge.

Charlés, L. L., & Samarasinghe, G. (Eds.) (2016). *Family therapy in global humanitarian contexts: Voices and issues from the field*. Springer.

Corey, G., Corey, M. S., & Corey, C. (2021). *Issues and ethics in the helping professions* (10th ed.). Cengage.

Coyle, S. M. (2022). *Spirituality in systemic family therapy supervision and training*. Springer.

de Shazer, S. (1982). *Patterns of brief family therapy*. Guilford.

de Shazer, S. (1985). *Keys to solution in brief therapy*. Norton.

de Shazer, S. (1988). *Clues: Investigating solutions in brief therapy*. Norton.

de Shazer, S. (1991). *Putting difference to work*. Norton.

de Shazer, S., Berg, I. K., Lipchik, E., Nunnally, E., Molnar, A., Gingerich, W., & Weiner-Davis, M. (1986). Brief therapy: Focused solution development. *Family Process, 25* (2), 207–221.

Ducommun-Nagy, C., & Reiter, M. D. (2014). Contextual therapy. In M. D. Reiter (Ed.). *Case conceptualization in family therapy* (pp. 55–81). Pearson.

Duncan, B. L., Miller, S. D., & Sparks, J. A. (2004). *The heroic client*. Jossey-Bass.

Epston, D., & White, M. (1992). *Experience, contradiction, narrative, imagination*. Dulwich Centre Publications.

Falicov, C. J. (2014). *Latino families in therapy* (2nd ed.). Guilford.

Fisch, R., Weakland, J. H., & Segal, L. (1982). *The tactics of change*. Jossey-Bass.

Fishman, H. C. (2022). *Performance-based family therapy*. Routledge.

Flemons, D., & Gralnik, L. M. (2013). *Relational suicide assessment*. Norton.

Gergen, K. J. (1991). *The saturated self*. Basic Books.

Gergen, K. J. (1994). *Realities and relationships*. Harvard University Press.

Gilbert, R. M. (2018). *The eight concepts of Bowen theory*. Leading Systems Press.

Gilbertson, J. (2020). *Telemental health: The essential guide to providing successful online therapy*. PESI Publishing.

Giré, A. P. (2022). *Online therapy stories*. Confer Books.

Gladding, S. T. (2018). *Family therapy: History, theory, and practice* (7th ed.). Merrill.

Haley, J. (1963). *Strategies of psychotherapy*. Grune & Stratton.

Haley, J. (1973). *Uncommon therapy: The psychiatric techniques of Milton H. Erickson, M. D.* Norton.

Haley, J. (1981). *Ordeal therapy.* Jossey-Bass.

Haley, J. (1987). *Problem-solving therapy* (2nd ed.). Jossey-Bass.

Haley, J., & Richeport-Haley, M. (2007). *Directive family therapy.* The Haworth Press.

Hanna, S. M., & Brown, J. H. (2004). *The practice of family therapy* (3rd ed.). Thomson.

Hanson, B. G. (1995). *General systems theory.* Taylor & Francis.

Hardy, K. V., & Laszloffy, T. A. (1995). The cultural genogram: Key to training culturally competent family therapists. *Journal of Marital and Family Therapy, 21,* 227–237.

Hartwell, E. E., Belous, C. K., et al. (2021). *Clinical guidelines for LGBTQIA affirming marriage and family therapy.* American Association for Marriage and Family Therapy.

Hecker, L., & Murphy, M. J. (2015). Contemporary and emerging ethical issues in family therapy. *Australian & New Zealand Journal of Family Therapy, 36* (4), 467–479.

Hecker, L., & Murphy, M. J. (2017). *Ethics and professional issues in couple and family therapy* (2nd ed.). Routledge.

Hoffman, L. (2001). *Family therapy: An intimate history.* Norton.

Hoyt, M. F., Bobele, M., Slive, A., Young, J., & Talmon, M. (Eds.) (2018). *Single-session therapy by walk-in or appointment: Administrative, clinical, and supervisory aspects of one-at-a-time services.* Routledge.

Hoyt, M. F., & Talmon, M. (Eds.). (2014). *Capturing the moment: Single-session therapy and walk-in services.* Crown House Publishing.

Keeney, B. P. (1983). *Aesthetics of change.* Guilford.

Keeney, B. P., & Ross, J. M. (1985). *Mind in therapy.* Basic Books.

Kelly, S. (2017). *Diversity in couple and family therapy.* Praeger.

Kerr, M. E. (2019). *Bowen theory's secrets.* Norton.

Kerr, M. E., & Bowen, M. (1988). *Family evaluation.* Norton.

Lambert, M. J. (1992). Psychotherapy outcome research: Implications for integrative and eclectical therapists. In J. C. Norcross & M. R. Goldfried (Eds.). *Handbook of psychotherapy integration* (pp. 94–129). Basic Books.

Madanes, C. (1981). *Strategic family therapy.* Jossey-Bass.

Madanes, C. (1984). *Behind the one-way mirror.* Jossey-Bass.

Madanes, C. (1991). Strategic family therapy. In A. S. Gurman, & D. P. Kniskern (Eds.). *Handbook of family therapy: Volume II* (pp. 396–416). Brunner/Mazel.

Madigan, S. (2011). *Narrative therapy.* American Psychological Association.

McDowell, T., Knudson-Martin, C., & Bermudez, J. M. (2018). *Socioculturally attuned family therapy: Guidelines for theory and practice.* Routledge.

McGoldrick, M., Gerson, R., & Petry, S. (2020). *Genograms: Assessment and treatment* (4th ed.). Norton.

McGoldrick, M., & Hardy, K. V. (2019). *Re-visioning family therapy: Addressing diversity in clinical practice* (3rd ed.). Guilford.

Miller, R. B., & Johnson, L. N. (2013). *Advanced methods in family therapy research.* Routledge.

Minuchin, P., Colapinto, J., & Minuchin, S. (1998). *Working with family of the poor.* Guilford.

Minuchin, S. (2012). *Families and family therapy.* Routledge.

Minuchin, S., & Fishman, H. C. (1981). *Family therapy techniques.* Harvard University Press.

Minuchin, S., Lee, W-Y., & Simon, G. M. (1996). *Mastering family therapy.* John Wiley & Sons.

Minuchin, S., Montalvo, B., Guerney, B., Rosman, B., & Schumer, F. (1967). *Families of the slums: An exploration of their structure and treatment.* Basic Books.

Minuchin, S., & Nichols, M. P. (1993). *Family healing.* The Free Press.

Minuchin, S., Nichols, M. P., & Lee, W-Y. (2007). *Assessing families and couples.* Boston: Allyn and Bacon.

Minuchin, S., Reiter, M. D., & Borda, C. (2021). *The Craft of Family Therapy* (2nd ed.). Routledge.

Napier, A. Y., & Whitaker, C. A. (1978). *The family crucible.* Harper & Row.

Neill, J. R., & Kniskern, D. P. (1982). *From psyche to system: The evolving therapy of Carl Whitaker.* Guilford.

Nelson, T. S., Chenail, R. J., Alexander, J. F., Crane, D. R., Johnson, S. M., & Schwallie, L. (2007). The development of core competencies for the practice of marriage and family therapy. *Journal of Marital and Family Therapy, 33* (4), 417–438.

Nelson, T. S., & Graves, T. (2011). Core competencies in advanced training: What supervisors say about graduate training. *Journal of Marital and Family Therapy, 37* (4), 429–451.

Nichols, M. P., & Fellenberg, S. (2000). The effective use of enactments in family therapy: A discovery-oriented process study. *Journal of Marital and Family Therapy, 26* (2), 143–152.

Norcross, J. C., Krebs, P. M., & Prochaska, J. O. (2011). Stages of change. *Journal of Clinical Psychology: In Session, 67* (2), 143–154.

Patterson, J., Williams, L., Edwards, T. M., Chamow, L., & Grauf-Grounds, C. (2009). *Essential skills in family therapy* (2nd ed.). Guilford.

Perosa, L. M., & Perosa, S. L. (2010). Assessing competencies in couples and family therapy/counseling: A call to the profession. *Journal of Marital and Family Therapy, 36* (2), 126–143.

Prata, G. (1990). *A systemic harpoon into family games.* Routledge.

Prochaska, J. O., & Norcross, J. C. (2001). Stages of change. *Psychotherapy: Theory, Research, Practice, Training, 38* (4), 443–448.

Prochaska, J. O., Norcross, J. C., and DiClimente, C. C. (2013). Applying the stages of change. In G. P. Koocher, J. C. Norcross, & B. A. Greene (Eds.). *Psychologists' desk reference* (3rd ed.) (pp. 176–181). Oxford University Press.

Rambo, A., Boyd, T., & Marquez, M. G. (2016). *The marriage and family therapy career guide.* Routledge.

Reiter, M. D. (2014). *Case Conceptualization in Family Therapy*. Pearson.

Reiter, M. D. (2018). *Family Therapy: An Introduction to Process, Practice, and Theory*. Routledge.

Reiter, M. D. (2019). *Systems Theories for Psychotherapists*. Routledge.

Rivett, M., & Buchmüller, J. (2017). *Family therapy skills and techniques in action*. Routledge.

Rogers, C. R. (1965). *Client-centered therapy*. Houghton Mifflin Company.

Rogers, C. R. (1989). The necessary and sufficient conditions of therapeutic personality change. In H. Kirschenbaum & V. L. Henderson (Eds.). *The Carl Rogers reader* (pp. 219–235). Houghton Mifflin Company.

Rogers, C. R., & Truax, C. B. (1967). The therapeutic conditions antecedent to change: A theoretical view. In C. R. Rogers (Ed.). *The therapeutic relationship and its impact* (pp. 97–108). Greenwood Press.

Satir, V. (1978). *Your many faces*. Celestial Arts.

Satir, V. (1983). *Conjoint family therapy* (3rd ed.). Science and Behavior Books.

Satir, V. (1988). *The new peoplemaking*. Science and Behavior Books.

Satir, V. (1994). You as a change agent. In V. Satir, J. Stachowiak, & H. A. Taschman. *Helping families to change* (pp. 37–62). Jason Aronson.

Satir, V., & Baldwin, M. (1983). *Satir step by step*. Science and Behavior Books.

Satir, V., Banmen, J., Gerber, J., & Gomori, M. (1991). *The Satir model*. Science and Behavior Books.

Selvini Palazzoli, M. (1977). *Self-starvation: From individual to family therapy in the treatment of anorexia nervosa*. Jason Aronson.

Selvini Palazzoli, M., Boscolo, L., Cecchin, G., & Prata, G. (1978a). *Paradox and counterparadox*. Jason Aronson.

Selvini Palazzoli, M., Boscolo, L., Cecchin, G., & Prata, G. (1978b). A ritualized prescription in family therapy: Odd days and even days. *Journal of Marriage and Family Counseling, 4*, 3–8.

Selvini Palazzoli, M., Boscolo, L., Cecchin, G., & Prata, G. (1980a). The problem of the referring person. *Journal of Marital and Family Therapy, 6*, 3–9.

Selvini Palazzoli, M., Boscolo, L., Cecchin, G., & Prata, G. (1980b). Hypothesizing—circularity—neutrality: Three guidelines for the conductor of the session, *Family Process, 19* (1), 3–12.

Selvini Palazzoli, M., Cirillo, S., Selvini, M., & Sorrentino, A. M. (1989). *Family games*. Norton.

Seponski, D. M., Bermudez, J. M., & Lewis, D. C. (2013). Creating culturally responsive family therapy models and research: Introducing the use of responsive evaluation as a method. *Journal of Marital and Family Therapy, 39* (1), 28–42.

Sprenkle, D. H., Davis, S. D., & Lebow, J. L. (2009). *Common factors in couple and family therapy*. Guilford.

Talmon, M. (1991). *Single session therapy: Maximizing the effect of the first (and often only) therapeutic encounter*. Jossey-Bass.

Talmon, M. (1993). *Single-session solutions: A guide to practical, effective, and affordable therapy*. Da Capo Lifelong Books.

Tomm, K. (1984). One perspective on the Milan systemic approach: Part II. Description of session format, interviewing style and interventions. *Journal of Marital and Family Therapy, 10* (3), 253–271.

Tomm, K. (1987). Interventive interviewing: Part II. Reflexive questioning as a means to enable self-healing. *Family Process, 26,* 167–183.

Tomm, K. (1988). Interventive interviewing: Part III: Intending to ask lineal, circular, strategic, or reflexive questions? *Family Process, 27,* 1–15.

Watzlawick, P., Bavelas, J. B., & Jackson, D. D. (1967). *Pragmatics of human communication.* Norton.

Watzlawick, P., Weakland, J., & Fisch, R. (1974). *Change: Principles of problem formation and problem resolution.* Norton.

Weakland, J. H. (2010). "Family therapy" with individuals. *Journal of Systemic Therapies, 29* (4), 40–48.

Weakland, J. H., Fisch, R., Watzlawick, P., & Bodin, A. M. (1974). Brief therapy: Focused problem resolution. *Family Process, 13* (2), 141–168.

Weinberg, H., & Rolnick, A. (2019). *Theory and practice of online therapy.* Routledge.

Whitaker, C. (1989). *Midnight musings of a family therapist.* Norton.

Whitaker, C. A., & Bumberry, W. M. (1988). *Dancing with the family.* Brunner/Mazel.

Whitaker, C., & Keith, D. V. (1981). Symbolic-experiential family therapy. In A. Gurman & D. Kniskern (Eds.). *The handbook of family therapy* (pp. 187–225). Brunner/Mazel.

White, M. (2007). *Maps of narrative practice.* Norton.

White, M. (2011). *Narrative practice: Continuing the conversations.* Norton.

White, M., & Epston, D. (1990). *Narrative means to therapeutic ends.* Norton.

Wilcoxon, A., Remley, T., & Gladding, S. (2013). *Ethical, legal, and professional issues in the practice of marriage and family therapy* (5th ed.). Pearson.

Williams, L., Patterson, J., & Edwards, T. M. (2014). *Clinician's guide to research methods in family therapy.* Guilford.

INDEX

Printed in the United States
by Baker & Taylor Publisher Services